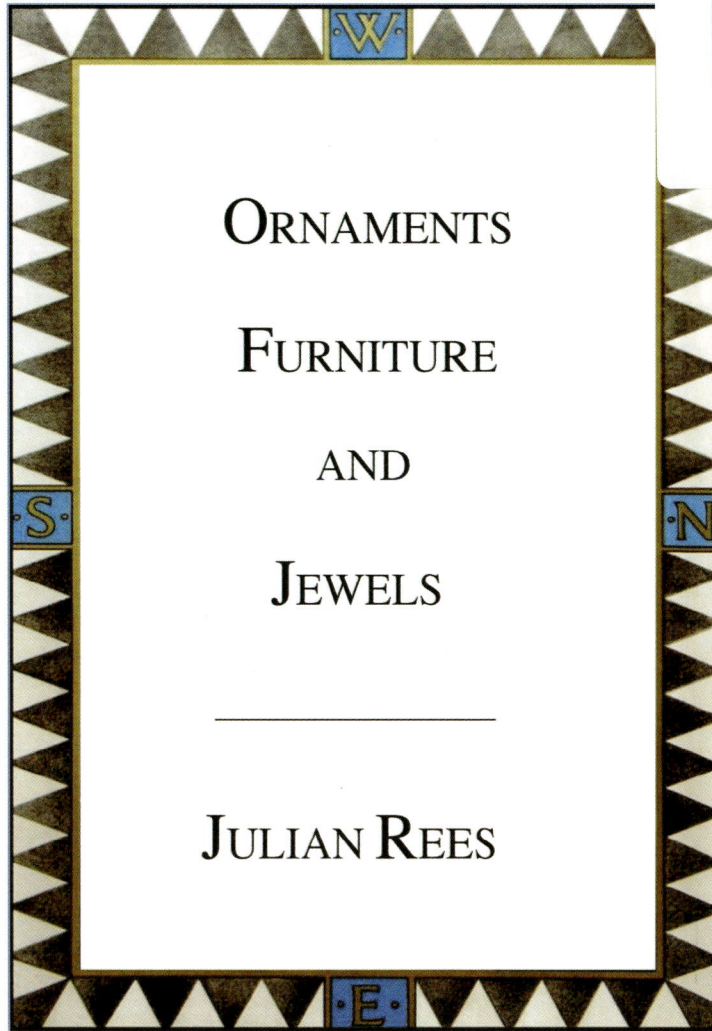

ORNAMENTS

FURNITURE

AND

JEWELS

JULIAN REES

First published 2013

ISBN 978 0 85318 412 6

© Julian Rees 2013

Published by Lewis Masonic
an imprint of Ian Allan Publishing Ltd, Shepperton, Middx TW17 8AS

Printed in England

Front cover: Cover design © Julian Rees

CONTENTS

ILLUSTRATIONS

80   upper: Early 19th century printed lambskin apron. *(Courtesy Chancellor Robert R. Livingston, Masonic Library of Grand Lodge, New York.*
Photo: Catherine Walter)
lower: Pre-1850 silk apron. *(Courtesy Chancellor Robert R. Livingston, Masonic Library of Grand Lodge, New York. Photo: Catherine Walter)*

81   upper: Leather apron, New York 1825-1850.
(Courtesy Chancellor Robert R. Livingston, Masonic Library of Grand Lodge, New York. Photo: Catherine Walter)
lower: Pre-1850 printed fabric apron.
(Courtesy Chancellor Robert R. Livingston, Masonic Library of Grand Lodge, New York. Photo: Catherine Walter)

82   upper: Hand-painted white silk apron, 1860. *(Courtesy Chancellor Robert R. Livingston, Masonic Library of Grand Lodge, New York. Photo: Catherine Walter)*
lower: Hand-painted silk French Master's apron, early 19th century. *(Courtesy Bibliothèque Grand Orient de France, Paris)*

83   Jewel of the first Master of Concord Lodge, New York, 1819.
(Courtesy Chancellor Robert R. Livingston, Masonic Library of Grand Lodge, New York. Photo: Catherine Walter)
lower: Compasses from the Kitchener Lodge. *(Courtesy Library and Museum of Freemasonry, London)*

84   upper: Past Master's Jewel of Benevolent Lodge, New York, inset with red and white stones. *(Chancellor Robert R. Livingston of Masonic Library, Grand Lodge of New York. Photo: Catherine Walter)*

85   Double-sided past Master's Jewel of Ocean Lodge, New York.
(Courtesy Chancellor Robert R. Livingston, Masonic Library of Grand Lodge, New York. Photo: Catherine Walter)

86   upper: 21st century plate of the Lodge Libération in Nevers, France. *(Courtesy Bibliothèque Grand Orient de France, Paris)*
lower: 21st century plate of the Lodge Libération in Nevers, France. *(Courtesy Bibliothèque Grand Orient de France, Paris)*

87   upper: French plate, 1831. *(Courtesy Bibliothèque Grand Orient de France, Paris)*
lower: Mid-18th century porcelain plaque depicting the tracing board, Moustiers. *(Courtesy Musée de Montluçon and Bibliothèque Grand Orient de France, Paris)*

88   upper: Cup in painted and gilded porcelain, 1858. *(Courtesy Library and Museum of Freemasonry, London)*
lower: Cup in gilded bohemian glass. *(Courtesy Library and Museum of Freemasonry, London)*

89   French Master's jewel from the 19th century onwards. *(Courtesy Bibliothèque Grand Orient de France, Paris)*

90   Rose windows in Amiens Cathedral. *(Photo: Jacques Trescases)*

91   upper: Detail from a window in Notre Dame Cathedral, Paris. *(Photo: Jacques Trescases)*
lower: Rose window in the Abbey of St. Ouen, Rouen. *(Photo: Jacques Trescases)*

92   Karlskirche, Vienna. *(Photo: Father Joe Koczera, S.J.)*

93   Lacquered mother-of-pearl inlay box. *(Courtesy International Order of Freemasonry Le Droit Humain, Surbiton. Photo: Julian Rees)*

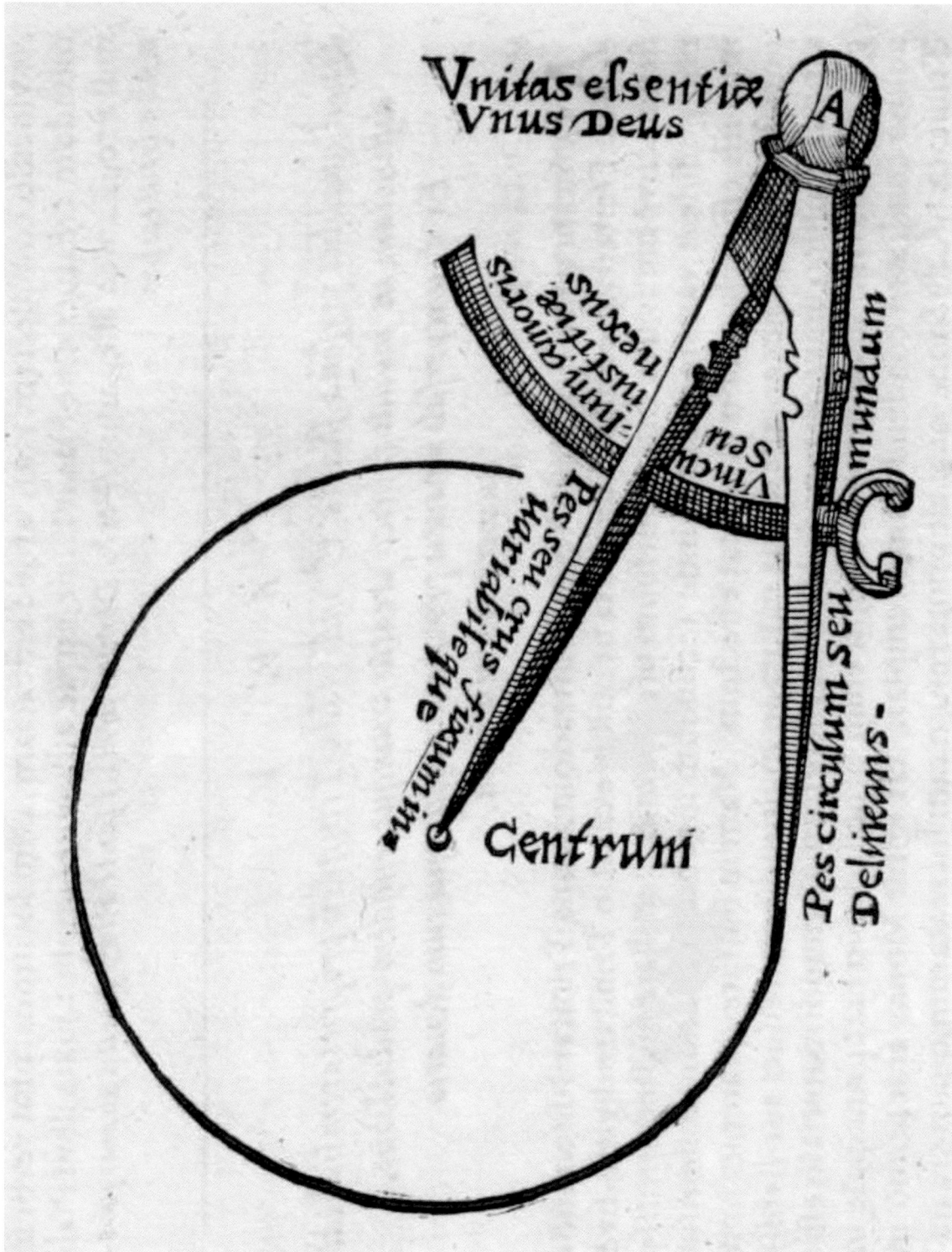

Sketch in Utriusque Cosmi Maioris by Robert Fludd, 1574-1637. For details see p.49.

ACKNOWLEDGMENTS

I wish to record my thanks to the following, all of whom have helped in different ways in the writing of this book: Michael Baigent; Martin Cherry, Mark Dennis and Alison Gardner of the Library and Museum of Freemasonry, London; Alun Graves of the Victoria & Albert Museum London; Ulrich Kneisl; Laziz Hamani; Irène Mainguy and Pierre Mollier of the Bibliothèque du Grand Orient de France, Paris; G. Hugh Milne, Provincial Grand Master of North Munster, Ireland; Thad Peterson of the Deutsches Freimaurermuseum, Bayreuth; Brian Roberts of the International Order of Freemasonry Le Droit Humain, Surbiton, Surrey; Tom Savini and Catherine Walter of the Chancellor Robert R. Livingston Masonic Library, New York; Dr Wolfgang Schneider and Dr Heinrich Mehl of Würzburg Cathedral; Prof Jan Snoek of Heidelberg University; Valerie Tougard of Editions Assoulines, Paris; Piers Vaughan of St Johns Lodge No.1, New York.

INTRODUCTION

Nowadays, in Lodges in many countries of the world, Freemasons are used to adhering to a plan of work sometimes set by the Lodge committee or council at the beginning of the year – a plan of work consisting of degree ceremonies. The installation of a new Master then takes place at the end of that year. Should that plan be upset by the absence of a candidate or, more commonly, by a lack of candidates coming forward, then a speaker is often invited, frequently from outside the Lodge, to speak preferably on a Masonic subject, although not exclusively so. In some Lodges, great importance is placed on the incoming Master striving to conduct, wherever possible, all three degree ceremonies during his year – preferably starting with the first degree, then the second and finishing with the third – to make a nice, neatly-planned programme of work. In some Lodges, if this is not possible and the Master only succeeds in working two of the three, the earliest opportunity is sought to allow him to work the 'missing' degree in the following year. Degree ceremonies seem nowadays to be foremost in the plan of work for the Lodge. This is a general rule; there are, however, Lodges where importance is placed on conducting non-ceremonial work.

All the evidence suggests that the practice of Freemasonry in the 18th century was very different from present-day convention. What records we have suggest a number of important differences: for one thing, we know that Lodges met much more frequently than they do today. We can get a sense of this from continental European Lodges, and Lodges outside of Anglo-Saxon Freemasonry, many of which meet once a month or more frequently. We also know that degree ceremonies were conducted less frequently: with 12 meetings a year, there were many held where there was no candidate for initiation. In any case, it was not uncommon for a candidate to be initiated *outside* of the lodge, and then brought to the meeting to engage in what was then far more important, the philosophical work in which Lodges commonly engaged. In many jurisdictions today, meetings will be dedicated to discussion and debate in which pieces of architecture are delivered and then commented on by the brethren, giving them the opportunity to expand their own knowledge and experience of Masonic principles.

Masonic flaming sword belonging to the Marquis de Lafayette, relief on gilt bronze with mother of pearl.

One of the most important differences in the 18th century was that once an aspirant had been initiated, he had to embark on an arduous course of study and work. He passed through various stages when the study he had undertaken was tested and his proficiency was assessed. If he had not made progress, if he had not arrived at the necessary level of competence, the aspirant was obliged to continue his study until he was considered competent. Only then could he be advanced to the next degree. Such a rigorous course of education meant that some months, or even years, might pass before the aspirant could advance to the next degree.

Another result of course was that the aspirant learned a great deal more than some of our candidates do nowadays. We can gauge some of this from the very incomplete references in our present-day ritual. For example, the questions leading from the first degree to the second in many English-language rituals contain the following exchange:

Q. Name the Grand Principles on which the Order is founded.
A. Brotherly Love, Relief and Truth.

We may well ask, how does the candidate know this? These three are nowhere mentioned in the first-degree ceremony! Similarly, when the candidate in the second degree has been invested with the second-degree apron, the Master addresses him as follows:

> *… as a Craftsman, you are expected to make the Liberal Arts and Sciences your future study, that you may the better be enabled to discharge your duties as a Mason, and estimate the wonderful works of the Almighty.*

But references to the liberal arts and sciences in the Emulation degree ceremony itself are very scant. The situation is much better in some jurisdictions, where a course of study is incorporated in the degree ceremony itself, as is the case in the International Order of Freemasonry Le Droit Humain. In the Emulation ritual a little later, the Master tells the aspirant:

> *… you are now permitted to extend your researches into the hidden mysteries of Nature and Science.*

When and where do aspirants have the opportunity to undertake such study? And yet, in the third degree, the Master tells him, in relation to the second degree:

> *The secrets of nature and the principles of intellectual truth were then unveiled to your view.*

We may search in vain in the Emulation second-degree ritual for any point at which such a revelation takes place.

The best conclusion we can come to about all this is that such considerations belonged, in former centuries, to the instruction, to the education of the aspirant. And indeed, when we look at the lectures worked in the Emulation ritual outside of the degree ceremonies, we find vestiges of such instruction where, for instance, grammar, rhetoric, logic, arithmetic, geometry, music and astronomy are fully defined and expanded upon.

Consider for a moment the following exchange:

Q. Have Masons secrets?
A. They have many invaluable ones.
Q. Where do they keep them?
A. In their hearts.

Q. As Masons, how do we hope to get at them?
A. By the help of a key.
Q. Does that key hang or lie?
A. It hangs.

Q. What does it hang by?
A. The thread of life, in the passage between guttural and pectoral.
Q. Why so nearly connected with the heart?
A. Being an index of the mind, it should utter nothing but what the heart truly dictates.
Q. It is a curious key; of what metal is it composed?
A. No metal; it is the tongue of good report.

Now we can see that well-worn phrase, 'the tongue of good report', in a completely different light. Consider also the following:

Q. On what ground do our Lodges stand?
A. Holy ground.

Q. Why on holy ground?
A. Because the first Lodge was consecrated.

Q. Why was it consecrated?
A. On account of three grand offerings thereon made, which met with divine approbation.

So, the ground of our Lodge is holy? What exactly sanctifies it? There are so many aspects to be discovered which the degree ritual does not address; yet it is exactly these aspects which our early brethren were exploring, in between conferring degrees.

This book explores the fifth section of the first Emulation lecture:

Q. Of what is the interior of a Freemasons' Lodge composed?
A. Ornaments, furniture and jewels.

You can read the rest of that section for yourself. Or you can come with us, as we go on a journey of exploration in this book.

1. THE POWER OF ALLEGORY

All the best fiction writing succeeds because the writer shows, depicts, decodes, by the power of words, a situation or an emotion without actually spelling it out. In Franz Kafka's novella *Metamorphosis*, the hero, Gregor, awakes one morning to find that he has been transformed into a gigantic beetle. His family don't know what to make of this; they end up ignoring him and shutting him in his room so that they may not be distressed by his appearance. Assuming that he cannot understand anything, no one talks to him directly, so he learns what is happening by listening to their conversations through the door. In the end, Gregor realises that his family would be better off without him and he decides to die. One interpretation of this story is as an allegory of how society tends to treat disability, disfigurement, incapacity of any kind; of how, for instance, people may tend to talk over the head of a person in a wheelchair. The power of the words drives the point home without actually mentioning the social conditions to which the story refers.

Depiction of the Blazing Star in a cast-iron grille, decorating the premises of the Grand Orient de France in Paris during the early 20th century.

Let us look at another example. In the film of Jane Austen's *Pride and Prejudice*, the two main characters, Elizabeth Bennet and Mr Darcy, have had a quarrel. Their differences, as we might imagine, are those of pride and of prejudice. But despite the apparently insurmountable differences between them, they are both secretly in love with each other, a love of which we, the audience, are as yet unaware. At a certain point in the film, both of them are invited to a soirée and are seated at opposite ends of the room. There is a certain amount of chatter going on; someone is playing the piano and so on. Darcy lifts his eyes to look at Elizabeth across the room. His look displays nothing but tenderness, and at the same moment her eyes meet his with a similar emotion. Nothing has been said to indicate that they are in love, yet for us, the audience, the import could not be clearer. But notice that it is for us to interpret that they are in love: nothing explicit is said.

In such a fictional situation, the author invites the reader to use his or her insight to decode or interpret what is going on. If we apply this to a Masonic context, on the Emulation first-degree tracing board, among other objects both explicit and implicit, there is a depiction of the sun. But the board also depicts the Blazing Star or Glory, a far brighter light source, inviting us to consider what light can possibly be brighter and more intense than the sun, the brightest known light source in the material universe. Now we can use our own insight in applying to this allegory a meaning that will fit with the rest of Masonic practice as it is known to us. Sure enough, sooner or later, we realise that the Blazing Star is representative of the divine presence and power of the Great Architect of the Universe Himself.

For us as Freemasons, symbolism and allegory are everything. So we should start with a quest. We have seen the above implicit examples of how a writer of fiction uses allegory. So what are allegories in the Masonic context? And why do we use them? As we have seen, an allegory is a narrative or pictorial representation of a subject under the guise of another subject, having certain points in common. We may also call it a symbolic representation. We use allegories as a way of engaging our own talents, our own insights, in revealing the meaning. With that knowledge, we may start to see how Freemasonry is full of allegories.

THE LODGE

We start with the first and most basic unit of Freemasonry – the Lodge. What is a Lodge? Is it a physical building? Not so, since by accepted Masonic practice a Lodge can be constituted, in exceptional circumstances, far away from a Masonic hall or Temple. We have only to consider examples of prisoners of war conducting Lodge meetings in their camps, or Lodges holding meetings in buildings that were not originally intended for Masonic ceremony.

We can view a Lodge as having three principal elements: the physical, the symbolic and the spiritual. The physical Lodge is most usually the room, Temple or building in which Masonic activity is undertaken. If, as is often asserted, our forebears were operative stonemasons who met in their lodges or workshops, then that building became the Lodge meeting place. But if early accounts are to be believed, that building only became a 'Lodge' by the practice of drawing emblematic symbols on the floor which the members wished to examine and interpret, and by the later practice of laying out a carpet or cloth on which these symbols were depicted.

Hence such a drawing or representation of the symbols seems to have been at least as important as, or more important than, the physical room or building in which the meeting was held. The drawing was an allegory of a Lodge. This brings us to the symbolic element of the Lodge, since such a carpet or floor cloth became itself known as 'the Lodge'.

The ground plan of this Lodge had to be due east and west. We can read about the reasons for this in the fourth section of the first Emulation lecture:

We never hear or read of any place being set apart for the public solemnisation of divine worship, until after the happy deliverance of the children of Israel from their Egyptian bondage, which it pleased the Almighty to effect with a high hand and an outstretched arm, under the conduct of His faithful servant Moses, according to a promise made their forefather, Abraham, that He would make of his seed a great and mighty people, even as the stars in heaven for number, and the sand of the sea for multitude. And as they were about to possess the gate of their enemies, and inherit the promised land, the Almighty thought proper to reveal to them those three most excellent institutions, namely the moral, ceremonial and judicial laws. And for the better solemnisation of divine worship, as well as a receptacle for the books and tables of the law, Moses caused a tent or tabernacle to be erected in the wilderness, which by God's especial command was situated due east and west, for Moses did everything according to a pattern shown him by the Lord on Mount Sinai. This tent or tabernacle proved afterwards to be the ground plan, in respect to situation, of that most magnificent Temple built at Jerusalem by that wise and mighty prince, King Solomon, whose regal splendour and unparalleled lustre far transcend our ideas.

Moses causing the waters of the Red Sea to part, permitting the Israelites to pass over to the Promised Land.

So the Master of a Masonic Lodge will sit in the 'east', although the building may not be aligned literally due east and west; in other words, the Lodge has designated the Master's place as a symbolical east and, allegorically, that is where he is seated.

The Emulation first-degree tracing board lecture tells us about the form of the Lodge:

> *The form of the Lodge is a parallelopipedon, in length from east to west, in breadth from north to south, in depth from the surface of the earth to its centre, and even as high as the heavens.*

The form of the physical Lodge is of a double cube, being as high as it is broad and twice as long. Later we will be referring to Hermes Trismegistus and the Emerald Tablet, in which we read the immortal phrase, 'As above, so below, to achieve the wonders of the One,' referring to the interaction of celestial and terrestrial domains, represented here by the double cube and later, as we know, in the second degree, by the two pillars on either side of the entrance to King Solomon's Temple, representing the celestial, or eternal, and the terrestrial, or temporal. Again, it is no accident that the proportions of the tracing board are themselves rectangular or double-square.

SYMBOLICAL REPRESENTATION

The Temple 'Johannis Corneloup' in the Grand Orient de France, Paris, during the early 20th century. Note the individual pattern of the Square Pavement.

With all this information, we have progressed from the concept of a Lodge as a physical entity to that of a symbolical representation, for this double-cubed form represents the duality in man's existence, namely the celestial and terrestrial realms, the unity of man's physical being within the eternity of the cosmos, an allegory which enlightens the whole Masonic path.

We have here what might be termed the 'shell' of the Lodge, namely the four walls, the floor and the ceiling. It is but an empty space, however, until we have furnished and adorned it. The layout of the Lodge may be accomplished by the inclusion of all the implements belonging to a well-furnished and well-decorated Lodge. So our symbolical Lodge is not quite complete – it yet lacks the interior emblems. As far as the interior is concerned, there are of course variations in custom and tradition between different countries and jurisdictions, and even between different Lodges in the same country. The basic implements, however, namely those without which a Lodge cannot properly operate are as follows:

Mosaic Pavement, also known as the Square Pavement

Blazing Star or Glory

Indented or tessellated border

Master's pedestal, which may also serve as an altar.
Ionic pillar by the Master's pedestal, the first of the lesser lights
Master's gavel
Altar, if Master's pedestal is not so used

Senior Warden's pedestal
Doric pillar by the Senior Warden's pedestal, the second of the lesser lights
Senior Warden's column
Senior Warden's gavel
Perfect ashlar on or near Senior Warden's pedestal

Junior Warden's pedestal
Corinthian pillar by the Junior Warden's pedestal, the third of the lesser lights
Junior Warden's column
Junior Warden's gavel
Rough ashlar on or near Junior Warden's pedestal

Tracing boards

Volume of the Sacred Law/Lore as the first of the three Great Lights
Square and Compasses as the other two Great Lights
Square, Level and Plumb Rule as jewels, and later also as working tools

Working tools of the degree that is being worked

THE TEMPLE
Let us consider that all of the objects listed serve as an allegory, and some of them as more than one. They will be unveiled as such in the following chapters. Another definition of a 'Lodge' is the assemblage of the brethren, working Masonically, so here we have three distinct definitions: the drawing on the floor, the building and the membership. The fullest of these three distinctions is probably the second, namely the building and its contents. This building is also known, in common with many places of worship, as a Temple.

The word 'Temple' is very interesting from a Masonic point of view. Freemasonry is not, of course, a religion, yet most Freemasons say prayers to the Great Architect and invoke His aid at the opening of a Lodge meeting and His blessing at the closing. It is therefore perfectly right and proper that the brethren refer to the space in which they dedicate themselves to Masonic pursuits – first among these being self-knowledge – as a Temple, a building regarded primarily as the dwelling place of God, or devoted to the worship of God.

The word 'temple' arose, in Christianity, principally out of the need to distinguish between the church as a building and the Church as the assemblage of Christians. Freemasons do not have that problem, since the assemblage of Freemasons is known as the Lodge and the building may therefore be designated the Temple. In the late 18th century, Protestant Christians began to use the word 'temple' to distinguish their place of worship from the churches of Roman Catholics. Each of the two ancient temples in Jerusalem was called *Beit Hamikdash*, which translates literally as 'the Holy House', and a Sikh temple is called a *Gurudwara*, that is 'the House of God'. The naming of places of worship in this way also substantiates the reference found in the fourth section of the first Emulation lecture:

Q. On what ground do our lodges stand?
A. Holy ground.
Q. Why on holy ground?
A. Because the first lodge was consecrated.

So here we have a space furnished with the implements we mentioned, in which there is a tracing board on which are depicted emblematic symbols which assist the Freemason in moralising on – and illustrating with allegory – features of his journey through life which will enable him to seek self-knowledge and perfection, moral growth and development. And what makes a Freemason's Lodge a sacred space is twofold: firstly that it is sanctified by the energy and power flowing at the opening of the Lodge; secondly, we may also regard such ground as having been sanctified by the actions of Freemasons over the years, possibly the centuries, that they have met there.

SUPPORTS

Apart from the tracing board, other features of the interior depict other such symbols. The three pillars are perhaps the most prominent and here is one of the richest allegories with which Freemasonry has been universally blessed.

Left to right: entablatures of the Ionic, Doric and Corinthian orders.

The fourth section of the first Emulation lecture enlightens us as follows:

Q. What supports a freemason's lodge?
A. Three great pillars.
Q. What are they called?
A. Wisdom, strength and beauty.
Q. Why wisdom, strength and beauty?
A. Wisdom to contrive, strength to support and beauty to adorn.

Note that there are three pillars supporting, namely wisdom, strength and beauty. We normally only think of strength as the necessary quality for support, yet here we have two qualities either side of it: wisdom and beauty. So allegorically, our building needs more than physical strength. It needs the other two qualities, so we are clearly talking about far more than physical support. It is a cogent lesson as to how, in the building of humanity in which Freemasons are engaged, wisdom of insight and beauty of expression are indispensable. Without them, the support will have no equilibrium: the building cannot stand.

In the fourth section of the second Emulation lecture, we are instructed in the rise of the orders of architecture, in particular the Ionic, Doric and Corinthian orders. The oldest of the three is the Doric. This is how Freemasons in the 18th century saw this order:

> *The Doric is the first of the Grecian orders and is placed second in the list of the five orders of architecture. Its column, agreeable to modern proportions, is eight diameters high. It has no ornament except mouldings on either base or capital. Its frieze is distinguished by triglyphs and metopes, and its cornice by mutules … The composition of this order is both grand and noble. Being formed after the model of a muscular, full-grown man, delicate ornaments are repugnant to its characteristic solidity. It therefore succeeds best in the regularity of its proportions and is principally used in warlike structures where strength and a noble simplicity are required.*

In other words, the whole concept of its design speaks of firmness, strength, sturdiness, robustness. Thus does the Senior Warden, whose column is of the Doric order, represent Hiram, King of Tyre, who is said to have supported King Solomon in the building of the Temple at Jerusalem with workmen and materials. Note that the proportions of the column were important considerations in designing orders of architecture; hence the height is exactly eight times the diameter, these proportions giving the column a sturdy aspect.

Compare this to the description afforded to the Ionic order:

> *At this era, their buildings, although admirably calculated for strength and convenience, wanted something in grace and elegance … This gave rise to the Ionic order. Its column is nine diameters high* [hence more slender than the Doric]*; its capital is adorned with volutes and its cornice has dentils. History informs us that the famous Temple of Diana at Ephesus* [Efes in modern-day Turkey] *… was composed of this order. Both elegance and ingenuity were displayed in the invention of this column. It is formed after the model of a beautiful young woman of an elegant shape, dressed in her hair, as a contrast to that of the Doric, which represents a robust, full-grown man …*

Example of the Ionic order, showing the characteristic scrolls and an application of the egg-and-dart design.

Indeed, if we look at the volutes or scrolls on either side of the capital we may see a stylised representation of a woman's hair. So with the Doric and Ionic columns we have a contrast: man and woman, strength and wisdom. This is not to say that strength is the sole province of men or wisdom that of women. The 'model of a muscular full-grown man' is used as an allegory of strength, whereas wisdom, needing no physical strength, is represented by an allegory altogether more elegant, polished, refined and pacific, and the proportions reflect this: the height is nine times the diameter, giving the column an altogether more slender aspect. But here we have a conundrum: what is it in the Ionic order, an emblem of femininity, which makes of it a suitable allegory with which to denote the Master of the Lodge?

It has been said that 'the Ionic column represents wisdom, and represents also the Master, because the Ionic column wisely combines the strength without the massiveness of the Doric'. But why the reference to the female gender? What might be the signification of that? The answer may reside in how gender plays no part in the function of the Ruler of the Lodge. It may refer to the duality in human nature, the fact that there is an aspect in each of us allowing both sides of our character, male and female, to play their role in the well-ruling and governing of the Lodge, and how gender plays little part in our journey on the Masonic path. And of course there are many Masonic jurisdictions worldwide which admit women, or are exclusively female in their membership.

As an interesting historical sideline, before the union of the two Grand Lodges in 1813 to form the United Grand Lodge of England, the Doric pillar was distinguished by the name of Wisdom and stood by the Master's pedestal, while the Ionic pillar was called Strength and stood by that of the Senior Warden. Clearly, a switch of allegories was found necessary at that time.

Pillars without something to support are really not much use. We have a clue to this when we read more into the fourth section of the first Emulation lecture:

Q. Why Wisdom, Strength and Beauty?

A. Wisdom to contrive, Strength to support and Beauty to adorn.

Q. Moralise them.

A. Wisdom to conduct us in all our undertakings, Strength to support us under all our difficulties, and Beauty to adorn the inward man.

Q. Illustrate them.

A. The universe is the Temple of the Deity whom we serve; Wisdom, Strength and Beauty are about His throne as pillars of His works, for His Wisdom is infinite, His Strength omnipotent, and Beauty shines through the whole of the creation in symmetry and order. The heavens He has stretched forth as a canopy; the earth He has planted as a footstool; He crowns His Temple with stars as with a diadem, and with His hand He extends the power and glory. The sun and moon are messengers of His will, and all His law is concord. The three great pillars supporting a freemason's lodge are emblematic of those divine attributes …

Q. As we have no noble orders of architecture known by the names of Wisdom, Strength and Beauty, to which do they refer?

A. The three most celebrated, which are the Ionic, Doric and Corinthian.

The covering of a freemason's lodge is later referred to as 'a celestial canopy of diverse colours, even the heavens'. And later in the same lecture we gain some insight from the biblical legend of Jacob, who had fled his parents' house after his brother had threatened to kill him. He journeyed in the desert and, 'being weary and benighted on a desert plain', lay down to rest:

> *… taking the earth for his bed, a stone for his pillow and the canopy of heaven for a covering.*

A canopy therefore protects and adorns at the same time and, as we later learn in the same lecture, it is the backdrop for the legendary story of Jacob's Ladder, featured on our tracing boards in the first degree:

> *[Jacob] there in a vision saw a ladder, the top of which reached to the heavens, and the angels of the Lord ascending and descending thereon.*

The ascending angels may be regarded as those taking our petitions to God, and those descending as bringing God's healing and sustaining grace to us.

SYMBOLISM IN THE TEMPLE

Returning to the symbolism of the three great pillars, we may regard those three qualities, wisdom, strength and beauty, as indispensable in the building, first of our own Temple and then, through that building, and in concert with our brethren in the context of our own Lodge, as indispensable in the building of the Temple of, and to, humanity at large. Spiritually also, the increase in wisdom to which Freemasons aspire is indispensable in guiding us towards perfection. Wisdom may be regarded as twofold: it is that which invokes a deep understanding, as a counterpoint to a breadth of information; it is also a capacity for

sound judgement and it is easy to see how these two definitions may work in harmony.

We will frequently need strength in the pursuit of perfection on our Masonic path. We will count on the support of the brethren around us, who lend us the strength of mutuality, the idea that our common strength is more than the sum of its several parts.

We will increase in inner beauty and will also honour the need to let that beauty shine in order to spread peace and harmony, qualities so often lacking in the world. Remember that we speak here not of the beauty of outward form or expression, so often held in high regard in the world around us. Yet for the aspirant, beauty also refers to that which is evolving, growing and maturing inside himself. Inner beauty, otherwise known as harmony and peace, is the fruit that may be ours on the journey.

And so supports of this kind become active mainstays of our Masonic pursuits on a broad plane. We will need those three principally, whatever other qualities we may bring into play while growing morally and spiritually. The allegories of these pillars, and the canopy they support, are very plain and easily decoded.

Altar in a lodge room of the Masonic Hall, New York, viewed from the east.

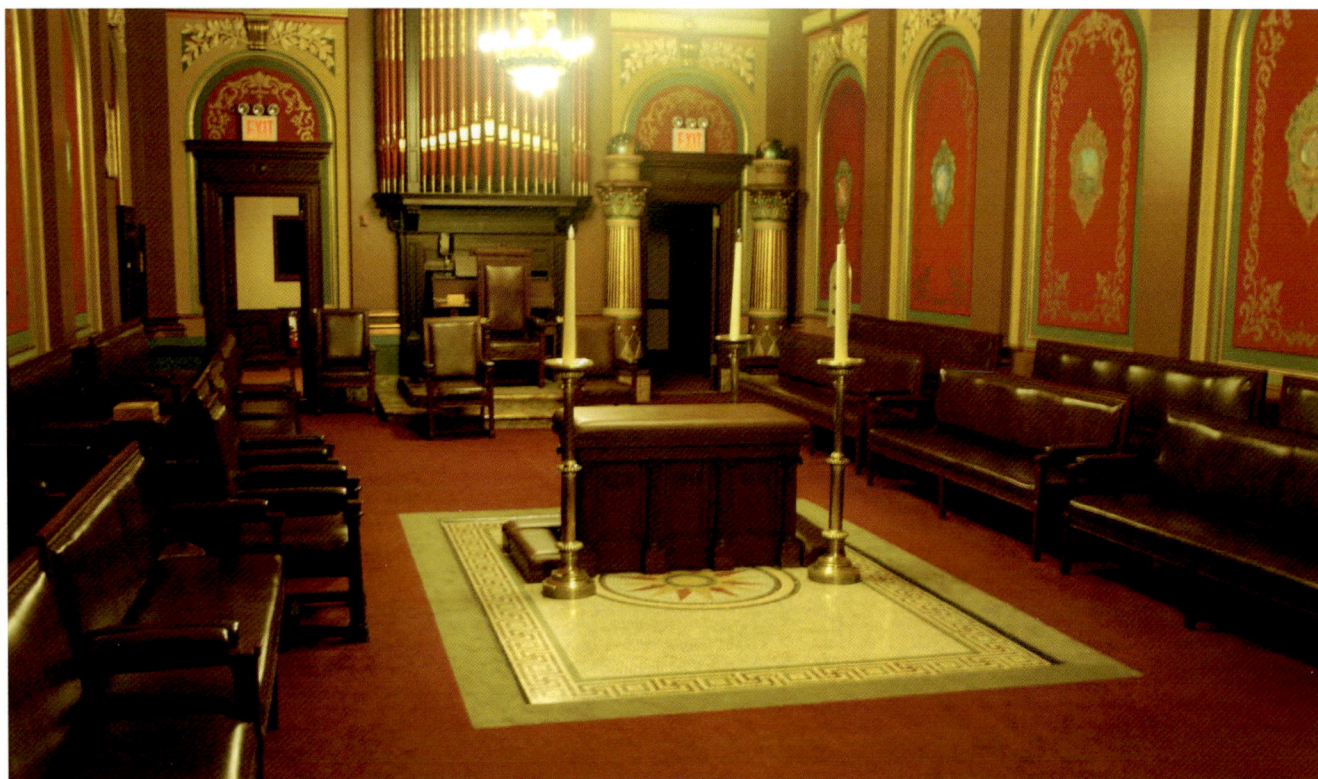

Now we come to some of the other accoutrements of a properly equipped Masonic lodge. Chief among these must be the altar. In many English Lodges, the Master's pedestal generally serves as the altar. Altars in ancient times were used for burning incense and for making sacrifices, to favourably incline the deity or indeed to appease it. There is evidence that in early English lodges in the 18th century no Bible or Sacred Volume of any kind was in use. However, since the earliest times altars have been invested with sanctity, so that a vow taken or a commitment made at an altar were always regarded as solemn and binding; hence the present custom in some Lodges around the world of taking a vow on the Sacred Volume at the altar.

In the United States of America and also in many countries outside of Anglo-Saxon influence or heritage, the altar is quite separate from the Master's pedestal, as indeed it is in many other jurisdictions. It is generally placed more or less in the centre of the Temple, two metres or more in front of the Master's pedestal, under the Blazing Star in some Lodges or under the Eternal Flame in others. The altar, or the Master's pedestal when used as such, is where the aspirant takes his obligation with his hand on the Sacred Volume and in this context it is a very sacred place.

The Master and the Wardens are of course the principal officers in the Lodge and the three pedestals therefore denote their relative positions and spheres of influence: the Master, situated in the east to open the Lodge and to govern it, is represented by the allegory of the rising sun. The Senior Warden, situated in the west to close the Lodge and to see that the brethren have received their wages, is represented by the allegory of the setting sun, the end of the day, the end of labour and, in some contexts, the end of earthly life. The Junior Warden, situated in the south, is represented by the allegory of the sun at midday, overseeing the brethren at labour and calling them from labour to refreshment and from refreshment to labour, as the situation demands.

Historically, the Junior Warden was not placed in the mid-south of the Lodge as he is today in many jurisdictions, but in the south at the west end of the Lodge; the Senior Warden was then placed in the north at the west end of the Lodge, so that the Wardens were placed on either side of the door of the Temple and each one flanked by his pillar, Doric and Corinthian. In this position, they were able to act as gatekeepers and the aspirant was admitted between the two pillars. The change in the position of the Wardens is quite unjustified: their proper positions are as gatekeepers, challenging the advance of any aspirant to test and see if he be worthy. The question 'Whom have you there?' has a challenging ring to it and was undoubtedly part of the ritualised way of disconcerting the aspirant before he was granted admission. The present arrangement of the Wardens has been in place for too long now. Too much water has flowed under the bridge and it will probably never be changed back, but note that some jurisdictions around the world still adhere to the configuration mentioned here: the Senior Warden in the northwest, the Junior Warden in the southwest, forming an isosceles triangle with the Master.

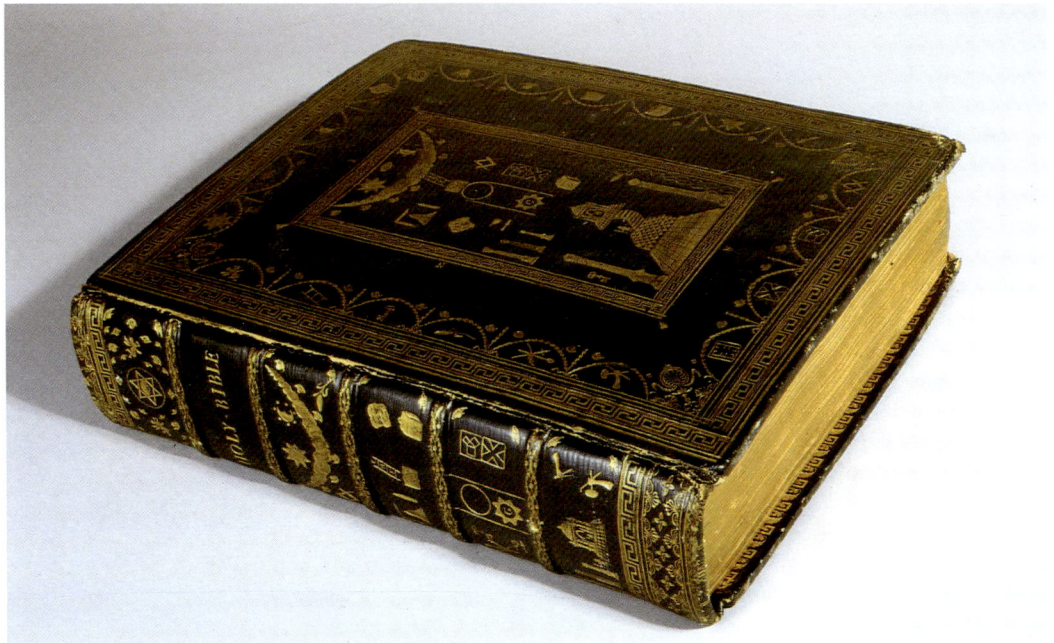

The Bible used as the Volume of the Sacred Law by the United Grand Lodge of England.

The last allegory we shall consider here before launching into our main study is the Sacred Volume. In some Masonic jurisdictions it is called the Volume of the Sacred Law, in others the Volume of the Sacred Lore. The difference probably resides in the view taken of the Divine Word – is it regarded as law imposed on us by the Almighty, as instructions having legal and dogmatic force, or is it 'lore' and therefore the body of traditional beliefs and anecdotes? In many Lodges in the world this volume is the Judaeo-Christian Bible, but importance is placed on the desirability of an aspirant entering into the Masonic vow with his hand on that sacred volume particular to his own religion. It has been argued that such a provision runs counter to the non-religious tenet of Freemasonry – a vow taken on one holy book should be as valid for a Freemason as that taken on another, merely by virtue of the fact that the vow is a solemn oath towards Freemasonry and its members, and as such embraces all religions. We will have more to say about the Sacred Volume in Chapter Three.

But the Sacred Volume represents both an allegory and the physical presence of God's will revealed to man. As such, it is the closest a Freemason comes, apart from prayers, to his acknowledgment of God as the Great Architect, guiding him in his journey along the Masonic path.

By now, you will have gained some insight into allegory, and what it can achieve and what we can achieve in our use of it. Keep all that in mind as we journey through the rich and varied landscape of Ornaments, Furniture and Jewels.

2. ORNAMENTS

The section of the Emulation lecture quoted in our Introduction begins:

Q. Of what is the interior of a freemason's lodge composed?
A. Ornaments, Furniture and Jewels.
Q. Name the Ornaments.
A. The Mosaic Pavement, the Blazing Star, and the Indented or Tessellated Border.
Q. Their situations?
A. The Mosaic Pavement is the beautiful flooring of the lodge; the Blazing Star, the Glory in the centre; and the Indented or Tessellated Border, the skirtwork round the same.

The ornaments, furniture and jewels of the Lodge have one thing in common: they are there to enhance and enrich, but each of these three groups does so in its own way. Each group comprises objects in the Lodge, each object having its own symbolism and significance, each inviting us to decode it to discover the precepts it illustrates, or can illustrate, once we have interpreted it in a Masonic context.

The second-degree tracing board flanked by two wallpaper designs by Victorian designer William Morris. It is clear that the designer of this tracing board, John Harris, was influenced by his contemporaries in its depiction of the tapestry-style coverings on the ground floor and first floor walls.

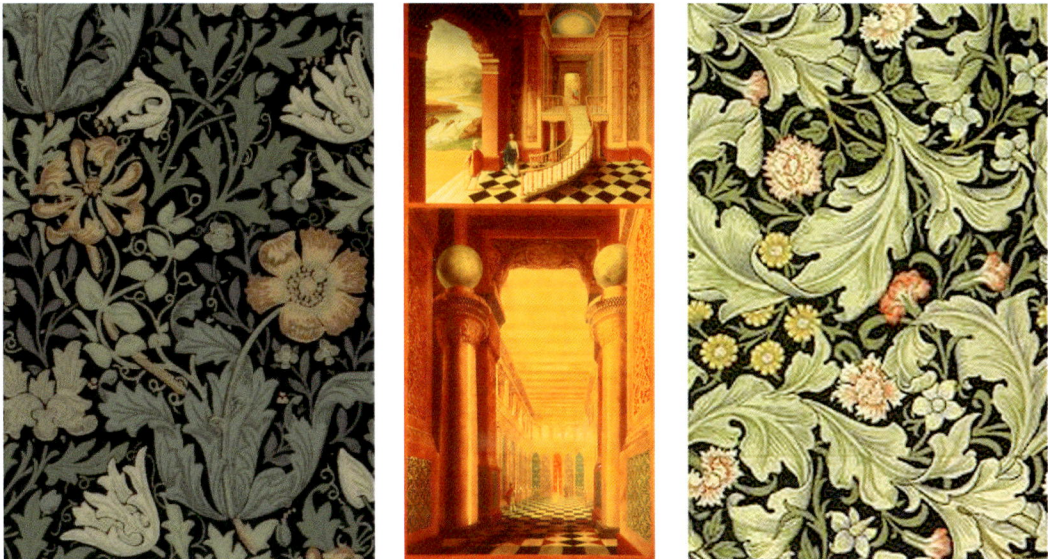

Ornamentation plays an important part in all artistic endeavours. A tapestry created as a wall covering or as draperies, curtains or upholstery, will frequently have exotic designs woven into it, or depict exaggerated scenes, fanciful and mythical beasts, exaggerated renditions of dramatic encounters, romantic scenes, battles and the like. The artist creates such exaggerations as a means of emphasising the subject matter he is depicting. In literature also, an event which might be considered mundane is embellished by the author in such a way as to emphasise the emotions of the characters. We can think of many examples of heroic deaths played out on the stage, particularly in opera, where the use of ornamentation in music will drive home the point the composer and librettist are trying to make. And at a very simple level, the composer will often introduce a trill played on two or more notes where a single note would have sufficed, simply to ornament it, making it more appealing even in a very gentle way.

THE PRE-RAPHAELITES

For us, the Romantic era in art, literature and music is very interesting. This was an intellectual movement that was at its peak in the period approximately from 1800 to 1850. It was a reaction to the Industrial Revolution but also to the Age of Enlightenment, the rationalisation of nature. It regarded emotion as an authentic source of aesthetic expression. Through this, art in antiquity was spontaneity in visual art and music. Through this, the exotic and the unfamiliar came to the fore in all forms of art and literature. All of this encouraged the individual imagination, and freedom from the stern classicism of the Age of Enlightenment.

The Romantic era gave rise to the Pre-Raphaelites, a group of English painters and poets whose aesthetic ideas launched a renewed interest in the Renaissance approach, particularly painting. Allied to this movement was the textile designer, writer and artist William Morris, 1834-1896, whose interior designs became iconic and are still widely in use today. Morris was influential in reviving traditional textile arts and production methods. One of his contemporaries, John Harris, 1791-1873, was the foremost designer of tracing boards in England and it is easy to see the influence of Morris and the other Pre-Raphaelites in Harris's tracing-board design. One has only to look at the wall coverings in the Emulation second-degree tracing board on the previous page.

Architects have long made use of ornamentation. Frequently we find ornamentation on the entablatures of columns,

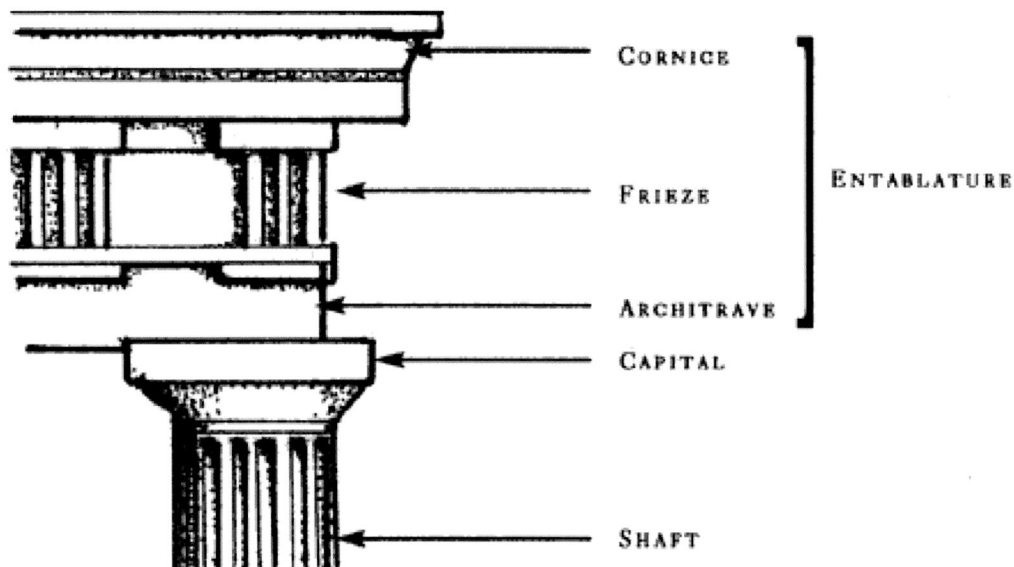

on doorways and window openings which may have been enriched with mouldings such as egg-and-dart designs,

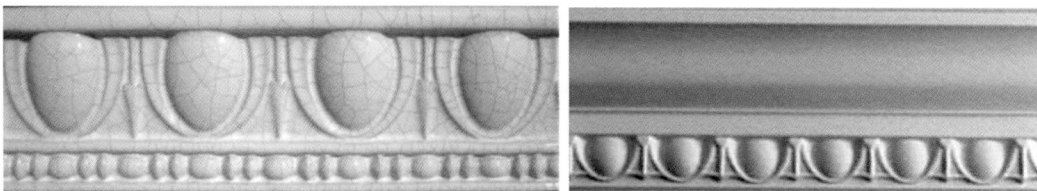

26

the anthemion petal design, frequently seen on Greek cornices,

and many more. One of the most common forms of ornamentation on pillars is fluting, which is sometimes used on the five orders in Freemasonry, except for the Doric order. The other four orders may display vertical flutes on their columns, although there are also many examples without it.

It is no accident that the third pillar in the lodge, the Corinthian pillar at the Junior Warden's pedestal, also the most elaborately ornamented of the three, is emblematic of beauty. It is worth repeating what we highlighted earlier:

> *Wisdom to conduct us in all our undertakings, strength to support us under all our difficulties, and beauty to adorn the inward man.*

In the fourth section of the second Emulation lecture, once the histories of the five noble orders have been illustrated and each order described in detail, we read the words:

> *Painting and sculpture strained every nerve to decorate the buildings fair science had raised, while the curious hand designed the furniture and tapestry, beautifying and adorning them with music, eloquence, poetry; temperance, fortitude, prudence, justice; virtue, honour, mercy; faith, hope, charity, and many other Masonic emblems, but none shone with greater splendour than brotherly love, relief, and truth.*

ADORNMENT AND SOMETHING MORE

But beauty and adornment come in many forms, some more elaborate and exotic than others. The first ornament in the Lodge, apparently very mundane and basic, is the Square Pavement, also called the Chequered or Mosaic Pavement. The word 'mosaic' has two meanings, each one in its way relevant to Freemasonry: mosaic ornamentation may be defined as the process of producing pictures or patterns by cementing together small pieces of stone, glass and so forth of various colours; but the second meaning, most relevant to us as Freemasons, is that 'pertaining or relating to Moses, the lawgiver of the Hebrews'. Hence 'mosaic law' was the ancient law of the Hebrews, contained in the Pentateuch of the Old Testament.

Interior of a lodge room in Freemasons' Hall, London, showing the Square Pavement.

At first sight the Mosaic Pavement, this ever-present object in our Lodges, shows us no more than a regular black and white chequer board such as is used in any number of games, from the most elaborate and sophisticated game of chess to the simplest game of draughts. For Freemasons, however, it represents far more. According to Masonic lore, the Mosaic Pavement is one of the indispensable elements of the Lodge. There are good reasons for this, for which let us again turn to the fifth section of the first Emulation lecture:

Why was mosaic work introduced into Freemasonry?
As the steps of man are trod in the various and uncertain incidents of life, and his days are variegated and chequered by a strange contrariety of events, his passage through this existence, though sometimes attended by prosperous circumstances, is often beset by a multitude of evils; hence is our Lodge furnished with mosaic work, to point out the uncertainty of all things here on earth. Today we may travel in prosperity; tomorrow we may totter on the uneven paths of weakness, temptation and adversity. Then, while such emblems are before us, we are morally instructed not to boast of anything, but to give heed to our ways, to walk uprightly and with humility before God, there being no station in life on which pride can with stability be founded; for though some are born to more elevated situations than others, yet, when in the grave, we are all on the level, death destroying all distinctions; and while our feet tread on this mosaic work, let our ideas recur to the original whence we copy; let us, as good men and Masons, act as the dictates of reason prompt us, to practise charity, maintain harmony, and endeavour to live in unity and brotherly love.

In the 18th and 19th centuries, aprons were often designed to show the Square Pavement in an Arcadian setting. This painted leather apron is possibly of Hungarian origin, dating from the early 19th century.

The illustration below is of a very individual design of pavement: a combination of squares and triangles made of small mosaic stones, placed at the entrance hallway of the Deutsches Freimaurermuseum in Bayreuth, Germany. It was the original flooring of the Lodge room from 1880 and was made by the firm Villeroy.

WHITE AND BLACK

White and black are, of course, exact opposites of each other; white is the total absence of pigment, black is the combined presence of pigments from across the spectrum. White is the sublime presence of unadulterated light in its purest form; black its complete absence. We often speak of the process of initiation as the passage from darkness to light, exactly as physical birth presents the same phenomenon. We can consider our condition before initiation as one in which we are in impenetrable darkness; initiation, with its insistence on the aspirant directing his gaze inward in order to know himself, will lead him from that very darkness to the light of self-knowledge. We therefore refer to our aspirant as 'a poor candidate in a state of darkness'. In the International Order of Freemasonry Le Droit Humain, one speaks of 'a blinded child of mortality seeking immortality'.

A state of darkness refers, on the superficial level, to the fact that the aspirant is blindfolded. But we also suspect, if we did not already know, that this is but an allegory of a deeper context. The aspirant may be 'in the dark' intellectually and spiritually. He may be 'in the dark' materially, physically and figuratively, since we have deprived him of the means by which he would be able to sustain himself in the world. He may, most importantly for us, be 'in the dark' as to his own true nature and his own true destiny. He needs light.

To progress towards the light we must *ipso facto* move away from darkness, move from unknowing to knowing, move from ignorance and fear to knowledge, harmony and wisdom, move from the black square to the white and, yes, from 'unborn to born'. A French ritual puts the matter in perspective, in the words the Master addresses to the aspirant just before the blindfold is removed:

*Prepare yourself to receive the light, not only that light which only falls on the eyes,
but a light more pure, which enlightens the spirit and enlivens the conscience.*

So in this sense, light, spiritual light, the grace of TGAOTU, is the nourishment which
our soul, our spirit, requires for its life, and that which ensures our conscience is functioning
properly so that we should not be tempted to abdicate our moral responsibility, in other
words so that our Plumb Rule remains upright, secured by a proper integrity. Remember
that each white square is surrounded by four black squares, reminding us of the ever-present
dangers: 'Today we may travel in prosperity; tomorrow, we may totter on the uneven paths of
weakness, temptation and adversity …' Remember also that, conversely, each black square is
surrounded by four white squares. The first of these two situations is a warning: when things
are going well, we are yet on the brink of misfortune. The second reminds us that, however
dark the place in which we find ourselves, be it physically, emotionally or spiritually, we
always have the opportunity to gain access to the light.

Before leaving the Square Pavement there is one more aspect we ought to consider. We
often hear it said that 'it's not all black and white', meaning that things are often not as
simple as they may appear. Indeed, we would do well to consider that when we are on a
white square, the black squares around us may indeed cast a shadow on what we are trying to
achieve. So as well as seeking the light and following that path which is properly illumined
for us, we should always be aware that what we are trying to do may be overshadowed by
contrary influences and we should be on our guard against them. Similarly, shadows may
conceal, so wherever we seek light we need to know what lurks at the periphery, in the
shadows, ready to unsettle our pursuits.

A STAR

We now come to the second of the ornaments, the Blazing Star, sometimes surrounded
by what is called a Glory. Originally the letter 'G' appeared on the earliest tracing boards
enclosed in a diamond shape;

later it was in the centre of a Glory, reminiscent of a flare,

or a comet. In fact the earliest depictions of the Blazing Star and the Glory together are of a 'G' within a comet;

A comet in 18th-century England was commonly known by the name of 'blazing star'. When the rituals were translated into French, the translator, unaware that the meaning was 'comet', translated it literally as *étoile flamboyante* or blazing star, when in fact he should have used the word *comète*. The comet referred to is the fabled 'star from the east' which is said to have appeared at the birth of Jesus Christ, to guide the wise men to the child. In the lectures credited to Thomas Dunckerley, the Blazing Star was said to represent 'the star which led the wise men to Bethlehem, proclaiming to mankind the nativity of the Son of God, and here conducting our spiritual progress to the Author of our redemption'.

Since the beginning of Masonic history the Blazing Star and Glory have been regarded as representative of divine presence and power. On modern tracing boards the Blazing Star is situated at the top of Jacob's Ladder and is therefore at the gateway to celestial realms. According to Browne's Master Key, the blazing star reminds us of …

> … *the omnipresence of the Almighty, overshadowing us with His Divine love and dispensing His blessings amongst us; and by being placed in the centre* [of the Lodge] *it ought to remind us that, wherever or however assembled, God the overseeing eye of providence is always in the midst of us, overseeing all our actions and observing the secret intents and movements of our hearts.*

What a far cry such images are from the resplendent ceiling in the Grand Temple of the United Grand Lodge of England in London:

We said that the earliest depictions of the Blazing Star were of a letter 'G' within a comet. In many Masonic Temples today there is a 'G' suspended in the middle, sometimes on its own, sometimes within a five-pointed star or a hexalpha. The letter 'G' is also found in many countries between the Square and Compasses united, and has thus become the principal symbol in Freemasonry.

Already in the 18th century, William Hutchinson wrote that to identify the letter 'G' with the name of God deprives it of much of its importance as a Masonic symbol. By its representation of God as the Grand Geometrician it represents geometry, 'which contains the determination, definition and proof of the order, beauty and wonderful wisdom of the power of God in His creation'.

Many depictions of the Blazing Star are surrounded by other emblems. The illustration on the following page is from a Temple in the Masonic Hall of the Grand Lodge of New

Blazing Star in the form of a letter 'G' within a hexalpha.

York, and shows two serpents either side of the Orb of Egypt. This represents the period in Ancient Egypt when man's awareness and level of understanding rose and developed from the earthly plane, looking toward a greater understanding on the heavenly and spiritual plane, symbolised by the serpents, representing attachment to the earth, and the wings representing man's aspirations soaring towards the heavens. The same symbolism is present in the illustration below: the Blazing Star in the Temple of the Order of Freemasonry Le Droit Humain, England. Here the serpents are clearly shown on either side of the Blazing Star, which is now in the centre of the Orb of Egypt, with the wings spread out wide on either side.

There is a further illustration of these serpents in the holder of the Eternal Flame at the same Temple.

BINDING TOGETHER

The third of the ornaments is the Indented or Tessellated Border:

> *The Indented or Tessellated Border refers us to the planets which, in their various revolutions, form a beautiful border or skirtwork round that grand luminary, the sun, as the other does round that of a Freemason's Lodge.*

In England we are used to a very simple, stylised black-and-white indented border, usually opposing triangles. Look at the Lodge carpet on page 39 for a markedly different arrangement. This border is in fact an adjunct to two separate items in the Lodge. It forms the border round the Mosaic Pavement and is therefore that which binds it together with the Blazing Star, emphasising the unity of the whole, the celestial world and the terrestrial united. This leads us to a consideration of the unity of God and man, reminding us of Renaissance alchemy. For this, we must digress for a moment.

In the middle of the 15th century, a number of documents dating from the medieval period all the way back to the writings of Plato found their way to the Court of Cosimo de Medici, whose family ruled Florence. These documents included neo-Platonic works from the second and third centuries AD. Some were written in an apparently Egyptian form, comprising the body of mystical literature which we today call the Hermetica. Marcilio Ficino, an Italian scholar, was convinced that these writings were Greek translations of the work of Hermes Trismegistus, the 'thrice greatest Hermes', believed to be an Egyptian contemporary of Moses. Ficino's translation revealed aspects common to Platonic philosophy and Christian doctrine. He was said to have believed that 'true philosophy and true religion, in other words Platonism and Christianity, must necessarily agree, since they both have their origin in the same source: in contemplative experience, or the inner relationship with God'. Ficino dedicated his life to uniting Platonic philosophy and Christianity.

Hermes Trismegistus was a legendary Hellenistic combination of the Greek god Hermes and the Egyptian god Thoth. In an alchemical text known as *The Emerald Tablet*, which claims to be the work of Hermes, we read:

> *True it is, without falsehood, certain and most true. That which is above is like to that which is below, and that which is below is like to that which is above, to accomplish the miracles of [the] one thing. And as all things were by contemplation [meditation] of [the] One, so all things arose from this one thing by a single act of adaptation. The father thereof is the sun, the mother the moon; the wind carried it in its womb; the Earth is the nurse thereof. It is the father of all works of wonder [Thelema] throughout the whole world. The power thereof is perfect, if it be cast on to earth.*

We do not have space here to go into a complete study, but the zealous student of allegory could do no better than to meditate on this fascinating text alone.

Hermes the Egyptian (Hermes Trismegistus), the legendary fount of alchemical knowledge. 17th century copper-plate engraving.

HERMES TRISMEGISTVS sive
TER MAXIMVS
Aegyptiorum Celebratissimus Philosophus Sacerdos
ic Rex omni genere doctrinae Instructissimus et Medici,
iae apud Aegyptios primus Inventor, vixit eo tempore, quo
Moyses natus.
Hermes omnia solus et ter unus M v. Martialis.

We mentioned earlier the double cube, said to denote man's dual nature: physical on the one hand, spiritual or Divine on the other. The spiritual or Divine side of his nature is an ethereal, non-physical counterpart to his physical body, governed by the same laws and inseparable from it. This duality embodies the principle quoted above in the extract from *The Emerald Tablet* which says 'as above, so below', just as Jacob's Ladder and the hexalpha are links between celestial and terrestrial domains. In this sense, Man is himself the archetype of a Lodge; in the same way that a physical Lodge is a coordination of different individuals, each one with his own characteristics, so each individual is a composite of the various properties which form his make-up. Just as a physical Lodge is characterised by the interaction of its various members, so the individual is characterised by the way his own faculties interact and by his state of spiritual awareness.

The tessellated border is also the border of the tracing board itself, binding all the symbols together. But on examination it proves to be more than this: at the corners are four tassels, denoting the four cardinal virtues of temperance, fortitude, prudence and justice. These four are also expanded upon in the lecture.

In French lodges there is a further representation of the indented border, in the form of a cord of union. This is a knotted rope passing right round the lodge at approximately shoulder or waist height and also depicted on some French tracing boards, giving us a more concrete example of the concept of that which binds us together. The knots can themselves be regarded symbolically on several levels, as we shall see. The cord will frequently end in tassels, reminiscent of the four tassels on the corners of the indented or tessellated border. We should also note in this regard the custom in many Lodges of the chain of union or chain of brotherhood, at the end of the Lodge meeting and after the Lodge is closed, when the brethren gather round the Mosaic Pavement, linking hands to form an unbroken chain and uniting for a moment in prayer or meditation when, for example, they may direct their combined energies towards a brother who is sick or in need, or towards relief in the case of a natural catastrophe.

So we have two principal ways of allegorically representing those sentiments which bind both the elements of Freemasonry and the Masonic brethren together: the Indented or Tesselated Border and the Cord of Union, the latter cord being both physical and figurative. But there is a third form of this allegory in Freemasonry, which is known as the Knotwork Pillar. Let us now spend a little time with columns.

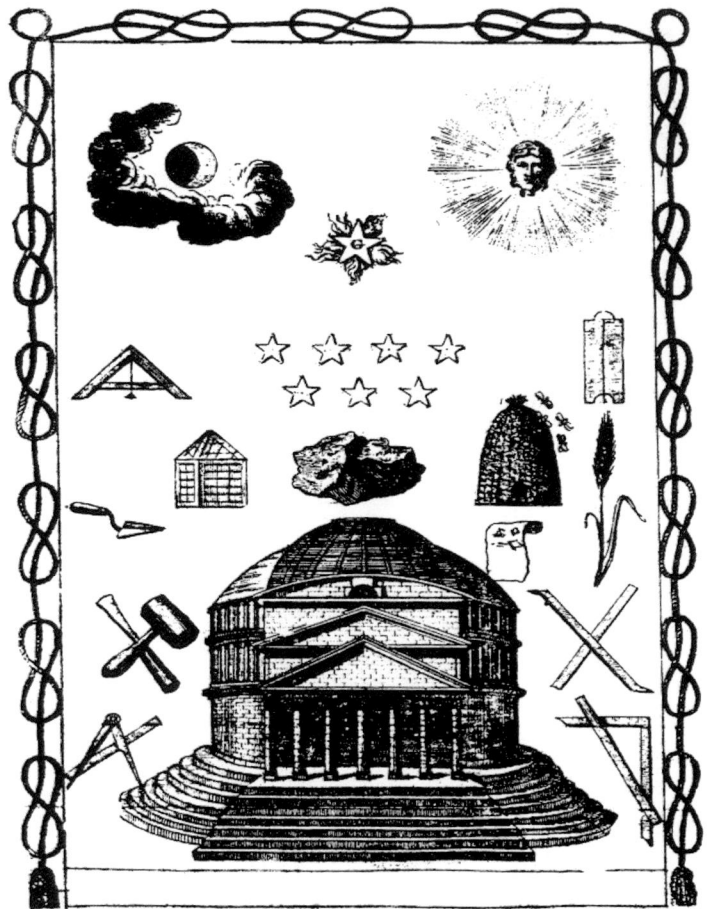

COLUMNS

The concept of two columns or pillars is a concept central to Freemasonry. We find so many instances of polarity, of dualism – sun and moon, day and night, divine and human, immortal and mortal, celestial and terrestrial, spirit and matter, soul and body, light and darkness, good and evil, innocence and guilt, female and male. Two columns can then be said to be emblematic of two independent and opposite principles.

In the 18th century, and still in some jurisdictions today, the proper situations of the Senior and Junior Wardens were at the northwest and southwest of the Lodge, thus flanking with their respective columns the entrance to the Temple and acting as gatekeepers. These two principal officers were there to grant, or refuse, admission to an aspirant. Here we have once again the opposition and duality: the Junior Warden representing the sun at midday, the Senior representing the moon at nightfall. Within this framework in continental European Freemasonry, the concept of a knotwork column makes its appearance fairly regularly, as seen below in an old Lodge carpet in Germany, dating from the mid-to-late 18th century.

Some of the best-known examples of knotwork columns are those found in St. Kilian's Cathedral in Würzburg, Germany, which at one time flanked the main portal, but today are rather less prominently situated outside the baptistery, without much light. The pillars bear the inscriptions engraved on the capitals of *Booz* for the pillar on the right – looking through the doorway into the baptistery – and *Iachim* for its partner. The Boaz pillar is shown as a group of four columns bundled together with two knots, the Jachin pillar as a group of eight columns with double knotting in the middle of the shaft. In Jachin the capital is also decorated with knots. Experts date these columns at circa 1230 AD and as such they count as the oldest examples of this curious art form. Compare this with the lodge carpet shown above, where the pillars are similarly arranged: Boaz on the right and Jachin on the left. Masonic ritual, however, conventionally refers to Boaz being the left-hand pillar and Jachin the right, and of course that is their situation when viewed from inside the Temple.

The naming of the columns comes from the reference in the Book of Kings to King Solomon's Temple in the Bible:

> *And King Solomon sent and fetched Hiram out of Tyre. He was a widow's son of the tribe of Naphthali, and his father was a man of Tyre, a worker in brass: and he was filled with wisdom, and understanding, and cunning to work all works in brass. And he came to King Solomon, and wrought all his work. For he cast two pillars of brass, of 18 cubits high apiece: and a line of 12 cubits did compass either of them about … And he set up the pillars in the porch of the temple: and he set up the right pillar, and called the name thereof Jachin: and he set up the left pillar, and called the name thereof Boaz.*

The Cord of Union spoken of earlier is a powerful binding symbol. One has only to think of the knotted rope used by monks and friars to bind their clothing. If we look again at the cords featured on the tracing board on page 38, we see that they are made up of loops or knots, another reminder of the power of unifying elements. If we apply these ideas now to the knotwork columns, we see that those very columns are nothing more than cords knotted together. If we examine the columns closely, we can also see that the individual ropes or cords they comprise appear to be endless – at best, they appear to spring out of the ground. Here then is an indication of infinity and the limitlessness of the union binding Freemasons together.

Above right: Knotwork pillars from Würzburg Cathedral in Germany, Right: Details of the knotwork. Bottom: inscriptions on the capitals.

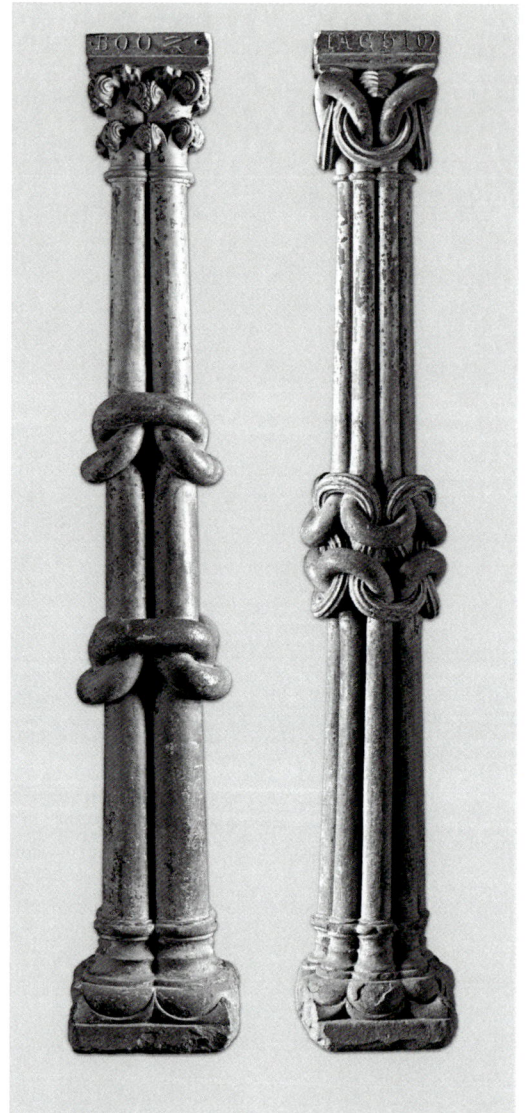

FURTHER ADORNMENT

So we have here the three universal Masonic ornaments, universal also in the sense that they apply to all three degrees. Once we progress from the first degree to the second, we find that these three are still present. The Mosaic Pavement, of course, can still be seen on the floor of the Lodge, but there are other depictions of this. Many early tracing boards show this ornament not as a square pavement but as triangular, diamond-shaped or as an even more intricate structure, as shown by the two illustrations on this page.

One of the oldest known tracing boards in existence, a lodge cloth from Austria dated at 1780, shows six horizontal rows each of black triangles interspersed with white inverted triangles, copying the normal pattern of the Indented or Tessellated Border. This was not unusual in the 18th and early 19th centuries. The same pattern occurs on the French tracing board of circa 1760 shown on the right and on Nordic Rite tracing boards of the same period.

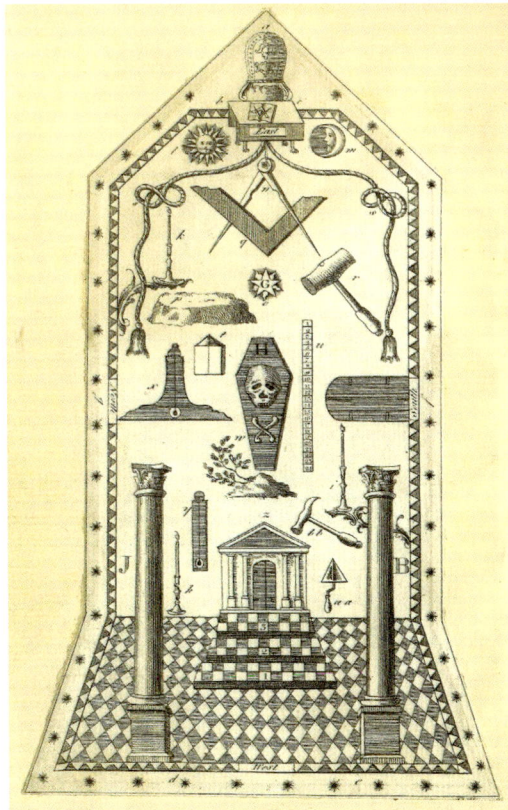

Still more common are instances of diamond form pavement, one of the earliest of which appears in the *Véritable Plan* (True Plan) of 1745 and in the exposure *Mahhabone*, published in 1766 and shown on the left. Other instances of this are John Cole's first-degree board of 1801, French second-degree boards of 1821 and, indeed, modern French boards.

Yet more intricate Mosaic Pavements than these are not uncommon. An early 19th-century board in the possession of Phoenix Lodge in England shows vertical rows of black diamonds on a white ground, alternating with rows of white diamonds on a black ground. Some early second-degree boards show a chequered pavement inside the middle chamber, while others show the pavement on the ground floor as well as inside the middle chamber. John Harris, the finest English tracing board designer, shows no pavement at all in his second-

John Harris's second-degree board of 1849, with a suggested scheme of the floor on the upper level. In the original Temple, these tiles would probably have been stone rather than ceramic.

degree board of 1820; in his 1825 board he shows a more intricate form on the ground floor only, with a standard chequerboard design on the first floor leading into the middle chamber itself. In his second-degree board of 1849, he shows a more or less standard chequerboard design on the ground floor and a more elaborate design in four colours on the first floor at the foot of the staircase. It is perhaps not correct to conflate these with the Square Pavement proper, but they form interesting examples of Masonic ornamentation.

SECOND AND THIRD DEGREES

In the second degree the Blazing Star appears, in English tracing boards, in the tympanum over the doorway into the middle chamber. The letter 'G' within it denotes Geometry, 'the first and noblest of sciences'.

We have noted certain differences between the ornaments of the first and second degrees, but basically those described here are common to all three degrees. However, when we progress to the third degree we find two more added:

> *The Ornaments of a Master Mason's lodge are the Porch, Dormer and Square Pavement.*

On the third-degree Emulation board designed by John Harris in 1845, we see depicted on the scroll across the coffin the interior of the middle chamber, with the dormer above. At the end, the porch and the veil provide the entrance to the Sanctum Sanctorum.

The Porch was the entrance to the Sanctum Sanctorum, the Dormer the window that gave light to the same, and the Square Pavement for the High Priest to walk on.

The Square Pavement appears to have the same connotation that it has in the other two degrees, and yet the traditional history, in describing the Sanctum Sanctorum, says that:

… nothing common or unclean was allowed to enter there, not even the High Priest but once a year, nor then until after many washings and purifications against the great day of expiation for sins …

so it is quite clear that the use of this Square Pavement in the third degree belongs only to those who have attained a higher level of spiritual consciousness, those raised by divine power 'to a reunion with the former companions of their toils', in another ritual rendered by the words 'to a higher life and a fuller knowledge of the teachings of our mysteries'.

TRANSITIONS

The other two ornaments are the porch which leads into the Sanctum Sanctorum and the dormer window, admitting light. The porch is in a very real but also allegorical sense a transition point, leading from the second to the third degree, and is similar to all transition points in Freemasonry. On entering the Temple at our initiation, as we know, we pass the greatest transition point in all Freemasonry: from unknowing to knowing; from the outside world into the sacred space of the Temple. On passing from the first to the second degree, we pass through the porchway at ground level in order to ascend the winding staircase before making another transition, namely into the Middle Chamber. The movement or displacement in the second degree, from ground floor to first, and the rotation through 90°, some say 180°, both entail a radical shift in perspective and an enduring change in our own insight, perhaps a change in our very character as we mature. This, of course, is another transition. But in the third degree we pass through the porch and into the Sanctum Sanctorum, to be united with God and with our own spiritual oneness, the most sublime transition of all.

Ornaments are there to adorn, yes. But they are also there to inform and to instruct. They are the rough stone on which we can try out our working tools. They will radiate beauty, but it is then up to us to discern and appreciate that beauty, and to interpret and employ it in our own Masonic progress.

3. FURNITURE

For us in the 21st century, the use here of the 18th-century word 'furniture' is perhaps a little incongruous. We are here not speaking of chairs, tables or sideboards. There are a number of dictionary definitions which may assist us: adornment or decoration is one and relates appropriately to the previous chapter; others include apparatus; tools; personal belongings; dress; apparel armour; accessory equipment; the movable, functional articles in a room or house. What we are doing is equipping our Lodge with those elements essential to our proper conduct in a space for Masonic work.

Collar jewel of the Grand Chaplain of the United Grand Lodge of England.

Q. Name the furniture of the lodge.

A. The Volume of the Sacred Law, the Compasses and Square.

Q. Their uses?

A. The Sacred Writings are to rule and govern our faith; on them we obligate our candidates for Freemasonry. So are the Compasses and Square, when united, to regulate our lives and actions.

Q. From whom is the first derived, and to whom do the other two more properly belong?

A. The Sacred Volume is derived from God to man in general; the Compasses belong to the Grand Master in particular, and the Square to the whole Craft.

Q. Why the Sacred Volume from God to man in general?

A. Because the Almighty has been pleased to reveal more of His divine will in that Holy Book than He has by any other means.

Q. Why the Compasses to the Grand Master in particular?

A. That being the chief instrument made use of in the formation of architectural plans and designs, is peculiarly appropriated to the Grand Master as an emblem of his dignity, he being the chief, head and governor of the Craft.

Q. And why the Square to the whole Craft?

A. The Craft being obligated within the Square are consequently bound to act thereon.

In most lodges in English-speaking countries, and in many others, the Sacred Volume, together with the Compasses and Square, form the three Great Lights. This holy book, known by some Freemasons as the Volume of the Sacred Law, by others as the Volume of the Sacred Lore, has long been an indispensable part of the Freemason's Lodge. In 1877, the Grand Orient de France allowed those who had no belief in the Supreme Being to become Freemasons. From then on, the presence of the Sacred Volume was left to the choice of individual Lodges in France and this, in part, led to the schism between the Grand Orient of France and the United Grand Lodge of England.

LANDMARKS

It is argued, in defence of the French position, that the definition of the landmarks is arbitrary and ambiguous, that Anderson's landmarks, recollection and interpretation of the historical landmarks are his own and that changes in both interpretation and practice have occurred before and since. In fact, the attitude of French society to the Catholic Church stems from the French Revolution, when it was held that there was no power higher than that of the people themselves. This was more an aversion to clericalism than to religion, but the effect of this has been, in the Grand Orient of France, to dissociate Freemasonry from institutional religion, underpinned by the law of 1905 separating Church and state, and enshrined today in the principle of laïcité, broadly speaking secularity, which in France governs attitudes towards religion. It therefore comes as a surprise to many English people to discover the tremendous spiritual, though non-religious, dimension to the practice of Freemasonry in the Grand Orient, despite the absence of a sacred volume.

In the United Grand Lodge of England, however, this Sacred Volume must be the Judaeo-Christian Bible, although other holy books, such as The Quran, The Vedas, The Talmud or The Bhagavad-Gītā, may also be present on the altar or Master's pedestal. Symbolically, the sacred volume is for the Master to impart the divine word to the aspirant and to the brethren in general.

KING JAMES AND THE BIBLE

Although, nowadays, sacred volumes of various different religions are used in Lodges, in the western world the Judaeo-Christian Bible is by far the most common. Amongst these, probably the King James Bible predominates, at least in English-speaking countries. There is plenty of evidence to suggest that before the Age of Enlightenment the Bible held little significance outside of religious practice;

in secular life it was not held in such high veneration in society at large as would become the case later in the 16th and 17th centuries. In 1611, however, King James I of England ordered that a new translation of the Bible should be undertaken.

The Bible had first been translated into English in the 14th century by John Wycliffe. But it was not until the invention by William Caxton of the printing press in 1476 that a printed version became available. Then, in 1523, during the reign of Henry VIII, William Tyndale became convinced that the way to God was through His word and that scripture should be available to common people, not just to scholars and the clergy. At that time the Church did not support any version of the Bible in English and, although Tyndale did succeed in printing his Bible on the continent of Europe and importing the copies into England, the idea was not welcomed. Tyndale was put to death in 1536.

Many of the expressions in Tyndale's Bible have passed through into the English language. The following sayings all have their origin in his translation: 'in the twinkling of an eye'; 'seek and ye shall find'; 'let there be light'; 'the powers that be'; 'my brother's keeper'; 'fight the good fight'; 'salt of the earth'; 'fell flat on his face'; 'a man after his own heart'; 'sour grapes'; 'pride comes before a fall'; 'the root of the matter'; and many more.

In spite of the original hostility to the idea of a printed Bible in English for the people to read, in 1539 Henry VIII officially authorised the publication of what came to be known as The Great Bible. During Henry's reign, the split with the Church in Rome took place and he appointed himself as the temporal head of the Church in England. Thus came about the Reformation in England, leading to the rise of Protestantism, as a result of which the use of the Latin language in church services was gradually abandoned.

But by the time of Henry's death in 1547, the King and his bishops had backtracked somewhat on the Reformation and forbade the reading of the Bible by ordinary men and women. After Queen

William Tyndale

Elizabeth came to the throne in 1558 that rule was relaxed and a number of Protestants who had fled to Switzerland composed, with the help of the Tyndale Bible, a new version which came to be known as the Geneva Bible. What makes this version significant is that, for the very first time, a mechanically printed, mass-produced Bible became available to ordinary men and women.

After Elizabeth's death in 1603 James I came to the throne, and it was considered that there were so many versions of the Bible in circulation that some attempt ought to be made to produce a standardised version, starting from a new translation. Accordingly, in 1604, the King selected 53 clergymen and one layman who formed six committees to undertake the translation. In fact, the King James Bible, as it came to be known, owes its largest debt to Tyndale's bible, published more than 80 years previously. But whereas many Bibles had merely translated from the Latin Bibles in use in Catholic churches, the translators went back to the original Hebrew in an attempt to come as close as possible to what had originally been set down in writing hundreds, and in some cases thousands, of years before then. Since the codification of the King James Bible, therefore, the sacred book has become much more an object of veneration.

And so it is that the Sacred Volume is held in veneration by most Freemasons throughout the world. In some American Grand Lodges and in the Grand Lodge of Scotland, there is an officer known as the Grand Bible Bearer. This officer carries the Bible on a velvet cushion in Masonic processions and at ceremonial occasions, such as the consecration of a new Lodge or in other public processions. This veneration is apparent also in private Lodges. When the Lodge is opened, the Immediate Past Master or the Director of Ceremonies opens the book and places the Square and Compasses on it in a configuration appropriate to the degree in which the Lodge is being opened. In some jurisdictions the brethren stand to order, the Immediate Past Master kneels in front of the altar, opens the book and arranges the Square and Compasses while the Deacons and the Director of Ceremonies cross their three wands

A silk apron with silk fringe and painted symbols from the early 19th century, showing the Bible open at Ecclesiastes chapter XII, appropriate to the third degree.

protectively over his head as he does so. In some jurisdictions, the first degree sign includes a movement reminiscent of the position of the hands under and upon the Sacred Volume when taking the obligation.

As far as ritual practice is concerned, it is sufficient to remember that the Sacred Writings are to rule and govern the faith of a Freemason. As such, Freemasons are urged to remember that those writings are God's revealed will to man and are the paramount expression of that. There has frequently been debate about the orientation of the Volume of the Sacred Law/ Lore. Should it be so placed that the Master may read from it, or the candidate? One view is that the Master is present to dispense the divine word to the brethren and that therefore it is he who should be able to read from it. This seems to be borne out by the words spoken after the installation of a new Master in the Emulation ritual:

The Sacred Volume, that great light in masonry, will guide you to all truth, direct your steps in the paths of happiness, and point out to you the whole duty of man.

This Bible is one of the most revered Masonic Bibles, known as the 'Washington Bible', printed in England in 1767. At that time copyright of the Bible belonged to the monarch, and although a few attempts were made to print illegal copies of Bibles in the colonies prior to independence, these were rare. This Bible belongs to St. John's Lodge No.1 in the State of New York and is the Bible on which George Washington swore his oath of allegiance as first President of the United States of America at his inauguration on 30 April 1789. At that inauguration, an equerry to George Washington was present, one Jacob Morton, who was also Master of St. John's Lodge. It is said that the page shown, the book of Genesis chapters 49 and 50, is the actual page on which he swore the oath, that following this he himself added the words 'so help me, God' and that he then kissed the bible in the middle of the cherubs on the left page. Tradition has it that the Bible was 'opened at random' but this cannot be substantiated. It is, however, true that all Presidents since have added the words 'so help me, God'. Those allowed to take their Obligation on the Bible nowadays are limited to Master Masons, the WM and Master-Elect of St. John's Lodge, the Grand Master of the Grand Lodge of New York, the Governor of New York State and the President of the United States. Due to its fragility and the fact that natural oils on hands can affect the vegetable dyes used in those days for ink, white gloves must be worn, with the sole exception of the President, who may use his bare hands.

ICONIC SYMBOLS

At the fulcrum:
Unitas essentiae – unus Deus
Unity of being – one God

On the circle segment of the dividers:
Vinculum amoris seu iustitiae nexus
A bond of love or a bond of justice

On the leg at the circumference:
Pes circulum seu mundum delineans
Foot on the circumference, or setting the world within limits

On the leg at the centre:
Pes seu crus fixum invariabileque
Foot or leg fixed and invariable

In the centre
Centrum
Centre

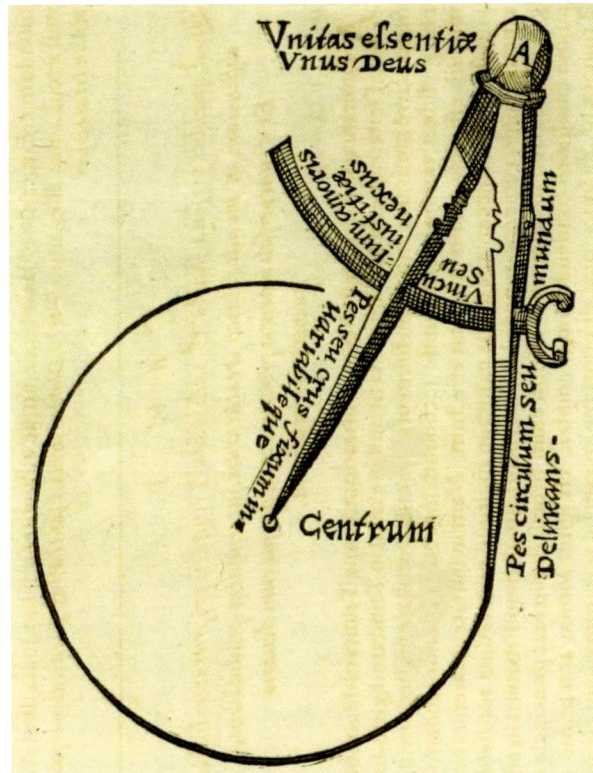

Sketch in Utriusque Cosmi Maioris by Robert Fludd, 1574-1637, astrologist and Paracelsian physician.

The Compasses form one of the most iconic and important implements used in Masonic ritual and practice. Together with the Square, they form the single most widely recognised Masonic emblem – the Square and Compasses. We can regard this combined symbol as the means of naming or marking a Freemason – his universally recognised badge, proudly worn and easily distinguished.

Image of Square and Compasses in the entrance hall of the Grand Lodge building in New York.

But if we look at it from another perspective, the Square teaches us about morals, about how our conduct towards others ought always to be 'square', that is, beyond reproach, always acting honestly and without evasion. At the same time the Compasses teach us to act within the limits of correct behaviour, exercising mutual respect and giving us the freedom to act as the dictates of conscience allow.

Then there is a further insight, deeper still, encompassing universal truths by which the Square represents balance, harmony, and the ability to play a part in the vast complexity which is humanity; the Compasses show that we are all guided by our own centre, a point at which we can be with ourselves and at peace. And it is learning to touch this point, to know this still, small point of harmony and balance, which is part of the true secret of Freemasonry.

We are dealing here with the Compasses and Square combined; these two implements also feature prominently in Freemasonry on their own. We will be looking at the Square in more depth in Chapter Four, when dealing with movable jewels, but it is worth mentioning here that the Square is the first of the three working tools in the second degree, the other two being the Level and the Plumb Rule. In operative building terms, the Plumb Rule assists in setting and maintaining uprights – no building whose perpendiculars are not properly established will be stable. The Level fulfils a similar purpose since, when floors, beams, lintels and window openings are not level, the whole structure will be 'out of kilter'. We do not often consider that a perfect level is at an angle of 90° with a perfect upright, reminding us of the exchange:

Q. By what implement in architecture will you be proved?
A. The Square.
Q. What is a Square?
A. An angle of 90°, or the fourth part of a circle.

Remember also the exhortation in the initiation ceremony: 'You are therefore expected to stand perfectly erect, with your feet in the form of a square, your body being thus an emblem of your mind and your feet of the rectitude of your actions.' So, the Square, the first of the working tools in the second degree, is the combination of the other two, the Level and the Plumb Rule. It is important also to remember the means by which an aspirant gains access to the privileges of the second degree: 'by the help of God, the assistance of the Square, and the benefit of a password'.

There is another dimension to the Square. J.S.M. Ward claims that the Square represents also the sun and the divine spark in man, and is therefore a divine symbol. One of the oldest depictions of the Square is as a 'gallows' square, that is, with one arm longer than the other. The Greek letter gamma, Γ, corresponds to Geometry and has of course a very important Masonic connotation.

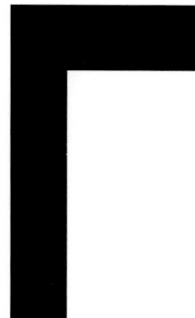

Γ

If we place two gammas together, we can form a rectangle, the form of the Lodge and thus a double cube:

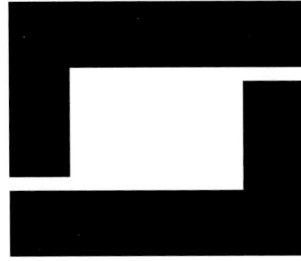

or if we place our four 'gallows' Squares together in another form, we can form a swastika:

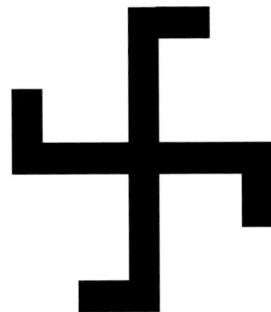

The swastika is a very ancient Sanskrit symbol dating back to the Indus Valley civilisation of ancient India. It is also found in classical antiquity and in many ancient civilisations around the world. It is still widely used today in Indian religions such as Hinduism and Buddhism as a symbol of auspiciousness, but also as a symbol of eternity.

The Compasses are also made use of not only as furniture but as one of the working tools, this time in the third degree. Operatively, the Compasses enable the skilful artist …

> … *with accuracy and precision to ascertain and determine the limits and proportions of [the building's] several parts.*

In a speculative sense, the Compasses …

> *… remind us of [God's] unerring and impartial justice, Who, having define for our instruction the limits of good and evil, will reward or punish as we have obeyed or disregarded His divine commands.*

But let us also examine the two explanations of the three greater lights. That in the first degree tells us:

> *The Sacred Writings are to govern our faith, the square to regulate our actions, and the compasses to keep us in due bounds with all mankind, particularly our brethren in freemasonry.*

In a working of the International Order of Freemasonry Le Droit Humain we read:

> *The Sacred Lore is to illumine our minds …*

We said earlier that the Square teaches us about morals, about how our conduct towards others ought always to be 'square'. But the Square here appears to be an active symbol – it regulates our actions and in this sense is no mere passive sign, reminding us of what it stands for; it is no longer only a part of the badge of a Freemason, but also a dynamic, an imperative. In the installation of a new Master we learn that …

> *… the square will teach you to regulate your life and actions according to the masonic line and rule.*

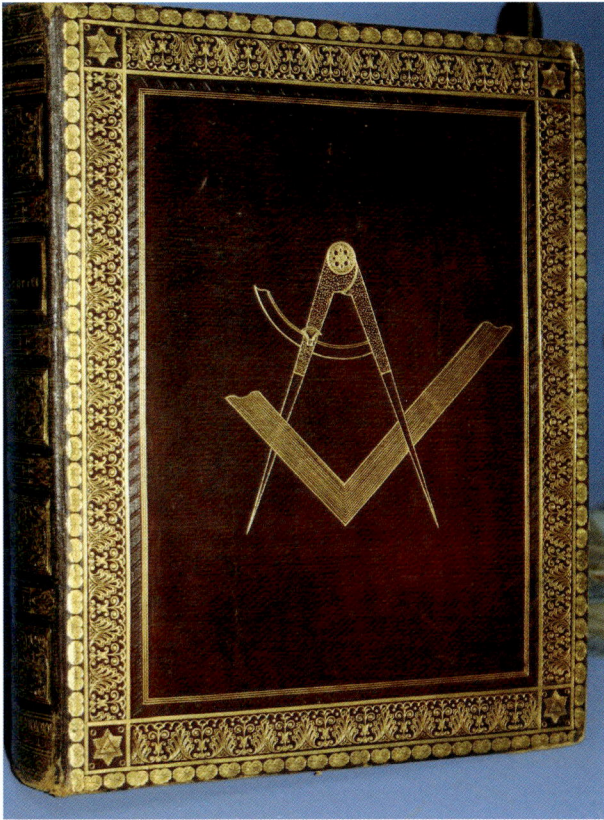

An old bible in
the Deutsches
Freimaurermuseum in
Bayreuth, Germany –
a representation of the
Three Great Lights and
the three elements of
the Furniture of the
Lodge.

There is a difference of emphasis also on the allegory of the Compasses. Again, in the installation of a new Master …

… the compasses remind you to limit your desires in every station in life …

So the Compasses, besides being there to 'ascertain and determine the limits and proportions of [the building's] several parts' or even to 'remind us of God's unerring and impartial justice', also have a more immediate significance and function: to keep us in due bounds with our fellow men, never to overstep the framework set by social custom and traditionally observed good behaviour and, in addition, to circumscribe our own desires and consequent actions. J.S.M. Ward speaks of the Compasses as having one arm at a fixed centre from which it never errs, namely God unmanifested. The other arm works around the circle, producing the emblem of the infinity of God, and is thus also an emblem of eternity.

And again, while considering these two implements combined, remember the means by which an aspirant gains access to the privileges of the third degree: 'by the help of God, *the united aid of the square and compasses*, and the benefit of a password'. So it is not merely these two separate implements which are there to sustain our aspiration: it is the union of the two by which we may arrive at a new, higher level of consciousness. They are not now some far-off emblem on the Sacred Volume, but are emblematically given into our hands as an allegory to aid us on our journey in this sublime degree, the Compasses now symbolically liberated from the constraints of the Square.

4. MOVABLE JEWELS

What is a jewel exactly? Why do we give the name 'jewel' to such diverse objects as a badge of office, a precious gem, a mineral stone used in a pivot in a watch, an article of adornment, a mark of distinction, a mark of rank, an object or even a person of great worth? There are many other uses of the word. But running through all of them there is a strand to do with luminosity, with enlightenment, with brilliance, lustre, radiance, brightness. And all of these, simply put, are aspects of – light.

Traditionally, the classification of jewels begins with a distinction between precious and semi-precious stones. In modern usage the precious stones are diamond, ruby, sapphire and emerald, with other gemstones being semi-precious. This distinction reflects the rarity of the respective stones in ancient times, as well as their quality. Most of them are translucent with fine colour in their purest forms, except for diamonds, which are colourless and very hard. Other stones are classified by their colour, translucency and hardness. To say that a jewel or gemstone is 'precious' or 'semi-precious' is misleading, in that it implies certain stones are intrinsically more valuable than others, which is not the case. It is all to do with the source and quality of that most essential property of a Freemason: light. Although we have dealt with light in relation to the Blazing Star, we are going to look at it now in a different context and see more than just a blaze of white or golden light.

Light is the transforming, revolutionising and transfiguring agent in our Masonic initiation. At the end of that part of the initiation ceremony in which the aspirant is deprived of sight, in England the Master asks, 'What is the predominant wish of your heart?' The aspirant replies, 'Light.' In a French ritual the Master gives a more direct injunction: 'Prepare yourself to receive the Light, not only that light which only falls on the eyes, but a Light more pure, which enlightens the spirit and enlivens the conscience.' And one of the most telling references to light must surely be that which is contained in the Gospel of St John in the Christian Bible:

> *In the beginning was the Word, and the Word was with God, and the Word was God. The same was in the beginning with God. All things were made by Him; and without Him was not anything made that was made. In Him was life; and the life was the light of men. And the light shineth in darkness; and the darkness comprehended it not.*

ISAAC NEWTON

There are plenty of light sources in the Lodge: the three great lights, the three lesser lights, the Blazing Star or Glory. And the traditional concept of a jewel, a precious stone or gem, is of the capability of reflecting and refracting light, and to do so in various colours according to the nature of the jewel. But how do we perceive light? What of the science of seeing?

In ancient times it was believed that sight was the result of light emanating from the eyes. In the fifth century BC, Empedocles put forward the theory that everything was composed of the four elements, namely fire, air, earth and water. According to this theory, Aphrodite made the human eye out of the four elements and lit the fire which shone out from the eye, making sight possible. We now know that the eye perceives light, either from its original source or from some object which refracts or reflects it.

But the nature of light was also misunderstood by the ancients. The Aristotelian concept was that light was white and that colours arose through its gradual modification. Red and yellow light, the colours of fire, were said to be modified the least. Green, blue and violet were said to be mingled with varying amounts of darkness.

Freemasonry, of course, arose in the Age of Enlightenment, an age when Isaac Newton was studying and lecturing on optics. He felt that this modification of light through prisms could be explained as a purely mechanical process and that a prism refracts each colour by a different amount. He described his discovery thus:

In the beginning of the year 1666 I procured me a Triangular glass-Prisme, to try therewith the celebrated Phaenomena of Colours. And in order thereto having darkened my chamber, and made a small hole in my window-shuts, to let in a convenient quantity of the Sun's light, I placed my Prisme at his entrance, that it might be thereby refracted to the opposite wall. It was at first a very pleasing divertisement, to view the vivid and intense Colours produced thereby …

Isaac Newton using a prism to analyse the colours in a ray of white light.

He demonstrated that a prism could decompose white light into a spectrum of colours, and that a lens and a second prism could recompose the multicoloured spectrum into white light. Newton also showed that the coloured light does not change its properties by separating out a coloured beam and shining it on various objects. Colour, he observed, was the result of objects interacting with already coloured light rather than objects generating the colour themselves. To students of such things in the 17th century, this was a true revelation.

For Freemasons, as we have seen, light symbolises knowledge; darkness symbolises its opposite, namely ignorance. Since jewels can both refract light and colour it, we should study them both as aids to Masonic symbolism and allegory and as aids towards the acquisition of knowledge and wisdom. In Freemasonry the word 'jewel' is used to depict a Square, a Level, a Plumb Line, an uncarved stone, a carved and polished stone and a tracing board. In other words, all of these objects shed light in some way: the light of knowledge. So we can regard all of these objects either as sources of light or as, in a sense, processors of light emanating from a separate source. But what makes these apparently mundane objects into jewels?

GENESIS OF MASONIC LIGHT

Working tools, serving also as movable jewels, in the Chancellor Robert R. Livingston Masonic Library of Grand Lodge, New York.

In this chapter we will deal with what are called movable jewels: the Square, Level and Plumb Rule. One of the most common mistakes made in interpreting Masonic ritual is to regard these three implements only as the working tools in the second degree – in fact they are far more important as the movable jewels in the Lodge, in all three degrees.

Let us look again at the fifth section of the first Emulation lecture:

Q. Before our ancient brethren had the benefit of such regular, well-formed, constituted Lodges as we now enjoy, where did they assemble?

A. On high hills and in low vales … and many other secret places.

Q. Why so high, low, and very secret?

A. The better to observe all who might ascend or descend; that if a stranger should approach, the Tyler might give timely notice to the Master, to hail the brethren, close the lodge, put by the jewels, and thereby prevent any of our Masonic secrets from being illegally obtained.

Q. You speak of jewels, and seem careful of them; how many are there in the lodge?

A. Three movable, and three immovable.

Q. Name the movable jewels.

A. The square, level and plumb rule.

Q. Their uses?

A. The square is to try, and adjust, rectangular corners of buildings and assist in bringing rude matter into due form; the level to lay levels and prove horizontals; the plumb rule to try, and adjust uprights while fixing them on their proper bases.

Q. It would appear from this that they are mere mechanical tools; why do you call them jewels?

A. On account of their moral tendency, which renders them jewels of inestimable value.

So here we have it: these apparently crude mechanical implements, whose face value seems to be no more than that of architects' or designers' aids, assume the quality of light-imparting and light-processing intermediaries, capable of enlightening the Freemason on his path, even of lending colour to the task he is undertaking. We may also speak of them in terms of their varying brilliance. They have indeed become, by Masonic allegory and thereby their moral tendency, 'jewels of inestimable value'.

To begin with the Square: as we have seen in the previous chapter, the Square has a very crucial role to play as a symbol when united with the Compasses. It forms, with the

A Square belonging to the New York Fireman's Lodge.

Compasses and the Volume of the Sacred Law/Lore, one of the three Great Lights. When united with the Compasses it becomes the indispensable aid by which an aspirant may move from the second to the third degree. But the Square on its own has most important symbolic aspects. Even before being introduced to its role as one of the three Great Lights, the aspirant, while still blindfolded, meets with this implement in his progress towards the Altar. Before progressing eastwards, the Junior Deacon instructs the aspirant to place his feet together and turn his right foot outwards to form a square. The aspirant then progresses, by means of three 'square' steps before kneeling, to take his obligation.

He may well be wondering what the significance of the Square is, but he will not have to wait long. After the Master has explained to him the dangers he has escaped and their significance, he proceeds to the communication of the secrets, preceded by the words:

> *… all squares, levels and perpendiculars are true and proper signs to know a Mason by. You are therefore expected to stand perfectly erect, your feet formed in a square, your body being thus considered an emblem of your mind, and your feet of the rectitude of your actions.*

So the shape of the square, as well as being an implement which forms a rigid and unchangeable angle of 90°, becomes then that symbol which will henceforth regulate the aspirant's life and

Detail of a brass Square dated 1507, found in the east corner of the north foundation of Baals Bridge in Limerick, Ireland, in 1830. The obverse inscription reads: I will strive to live with Love & care and the reverse reads: Upon the level By the Square.

actions. The rigidity of the angle demonstrates the rigidity to be adhered to in pursuit of morality and reminds the aspirant that deviation from the paths of moral rectitude ought to be as impossible as the deviation from the angle of 90°. It is not for nothing that the carpenter refers to this implement as the 'set-square' or 'try-square', or even 'true-square'.

When the aspirant comes to be passed to the second degree, he will hear the following exchange between the Inner Guard and the Tyler:

Q. How does he hope to obtain the privileges of the second degree?
A. By the help of God, the assistance of the square, and the benefit of a password.

His attention will thus be alerted to the fact that his progress will be facilitated by the degree of moral progress he has made since his initiation. And the Master acknowledges 'the propriety by which he seeks admission', a sort of validation of the aspirant's credentials.

PROGRESS

But now things start to become more elaborate. When the aspirant symbolically ascends the winding staircase, he takes five steps, each of them being part of a regular octagon. Each of these steps is not at an angle of 90° from the preceding one but of exactly half that, namely 45°. The aspirant will have to proceed by three steps in order to have completed an angle of 90°. How should we view this in relation to what we have discovered about the Square? It would seem that the aspirant, having been considered to have mastered the symbolism of the Square, is now exploring finer degrees, a means of more detailed progress. As we know, he is not merely progressing through a quarter-circle but he also ascending, a process requiring more caution, reminding us of that caution required of him at his initiation when rashness would symbolically have endangered his very life.

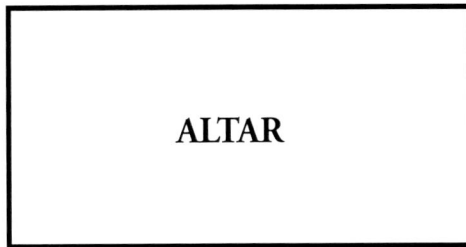

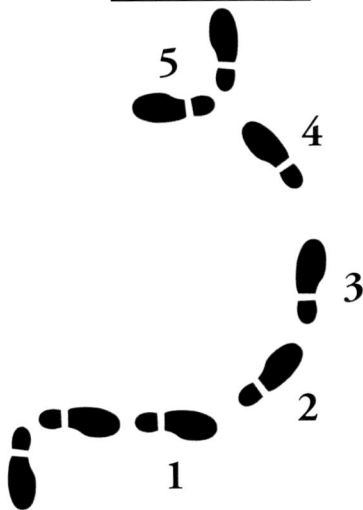

The aspirant's next encounter with the Square is in viewing the altered position of the Great Lights, when the Square partly yields to the Compasses, 'implying that you are now in the midway of Freemasonry' in the Emulation ritual, or 'implying that a new ray of light is now shed upon your life, which will enable you to discover the way to that wider knowledge to which, I trust, you will hereafter attain,' in the Lauderdale ritual. After this, Squares begin to appear in abundance: for example, in the sign of fidelity (two of them) and in the hailing sign (another two) whose other name, interestingly, is the sign of perseverance. The summation of all this is in the presentation of the working tools of the degree:

> *The Square is to try, and adjust, rectangular corners of buildings, and assist in bringing rude matter into due form … But as we are not all operative masons, but rather free and accepted or speculative, we apply these tools as symbols, and invest them with a moral significance …*

…confirming what was stated in the lecture quoted above. This lecture later illumines us with the following passage:

> *The Square teaches us to regulate our lives and actions according to the masonic line and rule, and to harmonise our conduct in this life, so as to render us acceptable to that Divine Being from whom all goodness springs, and to whom we must give an account of all our actions.*

LEVELLING AND INTEGRITY

Now we come to the symbolism of the Level. Whereas the Square in the operative sense checks angles in the building to ensure that they are true, the Level checks that the building blocks, stones or other materials, are set level, since a building whose foundation is not level cannot stand.

A Level of the Lord Kitchener of Khartoum Lodge No. 2767 of 1899.

… the Level to lay levels, and prove horizontals …

What the fifth section of the first Emulation lecture has to say a little later is of particular significance:

> *The Level demonstrates that we are all sprung from the same stock, partakers of the same nature, and sharers in the same hope; and although distinctions among men are necessary to preserve subordination, yet ought no eminence of situation make us forget that we are brothers; for he who is placed on the lowest spoke of fortune's wheel is equally entitled to our regard; as a time will come – and the wisest of us knows not how soon – when all distinctions, save those of goodness and virtue, shall cease, and death, the grand leveller of all human greatness, reduce us all to the same state.*

In fact, there is a very intimate relationship between the Level and the third movable jewel: the Plumb Rule. Let us listen now to how the lecture continues:

> *The infallible Plumb Rule, which, like Jacob's Ladder, connects heaven and earth, is the criterion of rectitude and truth. It teaches us to walk justly and uprightly before God and man, neither turning to the right nor left from the paths of virtue. Not to be an enthusiast, persecutor or slanderer of religion, neither bending towards avarice, injustice, malice, revenge, nor the envy and contempt of mankind, but giving up*

every selfish propensity which might injure others. To steer the bark of this life over the seas of passion, without quitting the helm of rectitude, is the highest perfection to which human nature can attain. And as the builder raises his column by the Level and perpendicular, so ought every Mason to conduct himself towards this world; to observe a due medium between avarice and profusion; to hold the scales of justice with equal poise; to make his passions and prejudices coincide with the just line of his conduct; and in all his pursuits to have eternity in view …

A particularly ornate collar jewel featuring the Plumb Rule.

In an operative sense, the Plumb Rule accomplishes a similar, complementary function to that of the Level: it is there to check that the building blocks, stones or other materials are set perpendicular. A building which advances in any other sense or direction than at 90° to the level base cannot stand. Note also that the lecture refers to the Plumb Rule as 'infallible'. Here we are once more back with Isaac Newton. Gravity ensures that a line suspended from above will *unerringly* hang perpendicularly. It sounds so simple that you would not think that this statement needs to be made, yet on such a statement rests the very principle of morality. It is 'the criterion of rectitude *and truth*' and teaches us to steer a middle way between exuberance and meanness. The builder does indeed 'raise his column by the level and perpendicular' and our conduct is guided by the same principles, to the point where we cannot, with a good conscience, stray from the paths of correct moral conduct towards others or spiritual conduct towards ourselves.

We mentioned that the Plumb Rule ensures that the building advances at an angle of ninety degrees to the level, and it is no accident that this is the same angle as that of the first movable jewel: the Square. Now we can see that the Square is the summation or perfect combination of the Level and Plumb Rule, so that the three will act and react in themselves and with each other, in perfect harmony.

We might pause here to consider another interesting feature of these, but now as working tools rather than as jewels. In the first degree, the working tools, 24-inch gauge, common gavel and chisel, are tools of preparation of the material: the means of making stones of the right size, the right shape and the right quality for the building. Here in the second degree, the working tools play no part directly in preparation but are rather tools of quality control. Now that the stones are prepared, the Fellow Craft uses the working tools of his degree to test that the finished product is fit to be used in the building. It does not take a great deal of imagination now, in applying our old friend allegory, to see how these can be used in the sense of advancement in our own moral growth and development.

MOVING ON

And why are these called movable jewels?

> … *because they are worn by the Master and his Wardens, and are transferable to their successors on nights of installation.*

We mentioned that these three jewels, taken together, work in harmony. So ought the principal officers to do so. The Master is distinguished by the Square, since …

> … *as it is by the square conduct of the Master that animosities are made to subside, should any unfortunately arise among the brethren, that the business of Masonry may be conducted with harmony and decorum.*

The Senior Warden is distinguished by the Level, since …

> … *that being an emblem of equality, points out the equal measures [he is] bound to pursue in conjunction with [the Master] in the well ruling and governing of the lodge.*

And the Junior Warden by the Plumb Rule, since …

> … *that being an emblem of uprightness, points out the integrity of the measures [he] is bound to pursue in conjunction with [the Master and the Senior Warden] in the well ruling and governing of the lodge …*

To sum up: the three movable jewels exist in a very intimate relationship with each other, a relationship where the Square is the summation or perfect combination of the Level and Plumb Rule. These three then are the principal aids in Freemasonry toward achieving moral growth and development.

5. IMMOVABLE JEWELS

To return for a moment to the lecture:

Q. Name the immovable jewels.
A. The tracing board, the rough and perfect ashlars.
Q. Their uses?
A. The tracing board is for the Master to lay lines and draw designs on; the rough ashlar to work,
mark and indent on; and the perfect ashlar for the experienced craftsman to try, and adjust
his jewels on.
Q. Why are these called immovable jewels?
A. Because they lie open and immovable in the lodge for the brethren to moralise on.

Tracing Board of
the Lodge of Unions
No. 256 circa 1801
(*United Grand Lodge
of England*).

Let us deal first with the tracing board. In almost every country in the world, Lodges have, or did have in the past, a tracing board or tressle board: *Tableau de Loge* in French, *Arbeitstafel* in German. This object can be in the form of a painting on wood, on cloth or even on leather, a black and white sketch, a woven carpet, and other forms besides. It is essentially *the Lodge itself* in a diagrammatic form, a *mappa mundi* of the symbols and allegories. They all seem to have taken their inspiration from the early custom among Freemasons of drawing on the floor of the lodge those symbols the brethren wished to expatiate on as their work for the evening in question. Here they were indeed 'moralising' on the symbols and allegories, hence the frequent practice of requiring the youngest, most newly-made Mason to start the drawing, which then not only tested his knowledge but also gave the opportunity to add to it, from inspiration within himself as well as from those around him.

Sculpture symbolising the transition from the rough to the perfect ashlar.

SYMBOLS

If we consider the first-degree board in different countries, there are certain features which are common to almost all and certain distinguishing features individual to certain countries or jurisdictions. Some features are not displayed on all the different types of first-degree board, but only on some of them. The table on the following page illustrates the point. Interestingly, the four countries mentioned all feature on their boards the Blazing Star or Glory, the chequered pavement, the 24-inch gauge, the ashlars, the cardinal points of the compass, the Square and Compasses, seven stars, sun and moon and the indented or tessellated border. French boards alone do not feature the Volume of the Sacred Law/Lore, reflecting the secular nature of society in France since the French Revolution. American boards are alone in featuring the All-Seeing Eye and the Book of Constitutions in addition to the Sacred Volume. Other peculiarly American symbols are the beehive, a symbol of industriousness, the pot of incense, the sword pointing at a heart and the winged hourglass. The Spitzhammer or pickhammer rather than the gavel and chisel is used in German rituals to work on the rough ashlar.

All of this testifies to the rich diversity of Masonic ritual across the globe, but also points up the features which are common and really important to most of them, as mentioned above. If we examine only those symbols, we find the core of Masonic allegory and symbolism, and those points

which unite all Masonic systems across the barriers of culture and language.

Thus the tracing board, the first of the immovable jewels, may justly be regarded as the core of Masonic teaching and practice. All of the elaborate and highly artistic examples are descended from that simple drawing on the floor made by our forefathers in chalk or charcoal in the 18th century, and probably much earlier than that. It is a fairly humbling thought that the symbolism which Freemasons use today comes down to us in an unbroken line from those early beginnings.

If we go back to the lecture we find some more enlightenment:

There is a beautiful comparison between the immovable jewels and the furniture of the lodge which I will thank you for.
As the tracing board is for the Master to lay lines and draw designs on, the better to enable the brethren to carry on the structure with regularity and propriety, so the VSL may justly be deemed the spiritual tracing board of the Great Architect of the Universe, in which are laid down such divine laws and moral plans, that were we conversant therein and adherent thereto, would bring us to an ethereal mansion not made with hands, eternal in the heavens …

In other words, if we examine and analyse the contents of the VSL we may find there divine laws and moral precepts which we may also find, in allegory and imagery, in the tracing board of the Lodge. The VSL has the capacity to instruct us in words with regard to the destiny sought for us by the Great Architect; in the tracing board we may come to study that destiny in allegory and to learn, by the power of our own spirit, heart and intellect, to interpret it and thereby to further our own spiritual progress.

To take concrete examples of this, think for a moment about the Blazing Star. This object should not be confused with the sun, also shown on the board nearby. It is much more appropriate to regard the Blazing Star, situated at or near the top of Jacob's Ladder, as the real presence of the Almighty, a light source brighter than any other in the universe, including that of our own sun.

The sun and moon, 'the one to govern the day and the other to govern the night', have a recurrent and very direct meaning for Freemasons:

	England	France	Germany	USA
24-in gauge	•	•	•	•
All-Seeing Eye				•
Anchor	•			
Ashlars	•	•	•	•
Beehive				•
Book of Constitutions				•
Cardinal points of compass	•	•	•	•
Cardinal virtues (tassels)	•		•	
Chequered pavement	•	•	•	•
Clock		•		
Cord of union		•	•	
Doorways north, south and west			•	
Faith, Hope and Charity	•			
Gavel and chisel	•		•	•
Glory	•	•		•
Jacob's Ladder	•			•
Key	•			
Moon	•	•	•	•
Pickhammer		•		
Pillars BJ (2)		•	•	•
Pillars, knotted (2)			•	
Pillars WSB (3)	•			•
Plumb Rule only			•	
Point within circle	•			
Pointed Cubic Stone		•		
Pot of incense				•
Square and Compasses	•	•		•
Square, Level and Plumb Rule	•			
Stars (7)	•	•		•
Steps only			•	•
Steps and doorway to temple		•	•	•
Sun	•	•	•	•
Sword and heart				•
Tessellated Border	•	•	•	•
Tracing board	•	•		•
Trowel	•			•
Volume of the Sacred Law/Lore	•		•	•
Windows east, south and west		•		
Winged hourglass				•

Q. The Master's place?

A. In the east.

Q. Why is he placed there?

A. As the sun rises in the east, to open and enliven the day, so the Master is placed in the east, to open the lodge, and employ and instruct the brethren in Freemasonry.

Think also of a similar reference in the exhortation to the new Master after his installation:

As a pattern for imitation, consider that glorious luminary of nature which, rising in the east, regularly diffuses light and lustre to all within its circle; in like manner it is your peculiar province to communicate light and instruction to the brethren of your Lodge.

So, the Master is there to employ and instruct, to communicate light and instruction, referred to here as 'light and lustre'. There are of course many other references to the sun. Think for a moment of the explanation of the three lesser lights in the first degree.

Printed mid-Victorian snuff kerchief showing the relationship between sun, moon, Blazing Star and All-Seeing Eye.

SUN AND MOON

It is of course the position of the sun, moon and Master that is being explained here, and the sun being in the south refers to the sun at midday and is therefore identifiable with the Junior Warden, who 'marks the sun at its meridian' or midday.

You are now enabled to discover the three lesser lights; they are situated east, south, and west, and are meant to represent the sun [in the south], moon [in the west], and Master of the Lodge [in the east]; the sun to rule the day, the moon to govern the night and the Master to rule and direct his Lodge.

What is the important dimension here in all these references? It is that of the Master *ruling and governing or directing* his Lodge. Let us be quite clear about this: a Master is present in his Lodge not to acquiesce to the general opinions, attitudes, views or judgements of the majority, but to rule, govern and, most importantly, to direct. Of course, a wise Master will listen to those around him but in the end he is the brother who, by virtue of his own accretion of knowledge and wisdom, will be in a position to *direct* his brethren who will, of course, in deference to his superior experience and wisdom, learn from him and obey his dictates. That is how Freemasonry operates and it is no different from the ancient operative masons whose masters so governed their charges, apprentices or fellows in their best interests. That is the basis of all happy and fruitful working arrangements, and Freemasons do well to remember this.

ARCHITECTURE.

A Comparative View of the Five Orders of Architecture.

Remember, too, the three orders of architecture which adorn the three principal officers of the Lodge. The Master is distinguished by the Ionic order, denoting wisdom, the Senior Warden by the Doric order, denoting strength and the Junior Warden by the Corinthian order, denoting beauty. And it is no accident that the Master's quality, namely that of wisdom, is so closely connected with the brightest light source known in our universe, namely the sun. So should wisdom shine and be a beacon for all Freemasons through their Master, the brother selected by the brethren of the lodge to be their ruler.

Next we come to the moon, the sun's pale sister, whose dull, lustreless, pallid light is but a poor copy of her brother's glorious effulgence and brilliant rays. According to the passage of ritual quoted above, the moon governs the night and is therefore placed in the west, that point of the compass where the sun sets. Consider this:

Q. Brother Senior Warden, your place in the lodge?
A. In the west.
Q. Why are you placed there?
A. To mark the setting sun, to close the lodge by command of the Master, after having seen that every brother has had his due.

The sun, rising in the east, opens the day: the Master placed in the east opens the Lodge. Both of them are there to launch something but, as we have seen, it is more than that: they are there to impart light and the Master's light is, of course, that allegorical light through which we may all become Freemasons. The sun, setting in the west, closes the day: the Senior Warden placed in the west closes the Lodge. Both of them are there to bring something to a close. But there are some more words, dealing with something more than just ends and closure:

… after having seen that every brother has had his due.

So the Senior Warden's duty, or more correctly, one of his duties, is to ensure that payment and recompense is made for work done. As we know, this is spiritual work upon our innermost being and so the recompense will likewise be reward of a spiritual nature, growing straight and seeing the effects on ourselves of the spiritual progress we have made as a result of Masonic labour.

Depiction of the sun and moon in a temple of the International Order of Freemasonry in Paris.

There is another dimension to the subject of the sun and moon. As we know, the first degree is the passage from darkness to light and as such is rightly regarded as an allegory of birth. The rising of the sun is a similar passage from darkness to light. In like manner, when we consider the allegory of the setting sun, we are immediately transported into the realms of the third degree: the sun setting in the west, giving place to the moon which governs the night, is also the emblem of the end of physical life and the transition to life eternal. And just as the Master's column, being of the Ionic order, denotes wisdom, so the Senior Warden's column, being of the Doric order, denotes strength in many forms, including surely that strength needed when faced with death and transfiguration, strength when faced with metamorphosis into a new state of being. The light of the sun has gone. The glimmering ray symbolises the continuing presence of the Master even at the last hour, and symbolises also the teaching of the Master. As Colin Dyer puts it in *Symbolism in Craft Fremasonry*:

> As the Master was present in the lodge, his light remained, as the spiritual and moral teaching which he gave would still be with a brother at the time of death, although those grand luminaries, the sun and moon, would no longer be of use to him. By the help of this teaching, he would triumph over death and succeed to life eternal …

But, and this is important, the light given to us at our initiation stays with us through life. As the first degree is the degree of birth, so the second degree is the degree of life and life's journey, symbolised by the Junior Warden and his Corinthian column, denoting beauty. And the strength needed when death calls us from our earthly labours is provided by the Doric column at the Senior Warden's pedestal. The power of allegory at work!

SEVEN STARS

Schinkel's design for Act One Scene Six of Mozart's opera *The Magic Flute* has a consonance with the Masonic ritual which refers to the covering of a Freemason's lodge being 'a celestial canopy of diverse colours, even the heavens'.

The next symbol on the tracing board, which is common to practically all countries and jurisdictions, is that of the stars, most commonly seven in number and normally found in a group situated on the tracing board between the sun and moon. This number of seven stars is found in a great many contexts dating from antiquity. Let us begin with the Masonic connection and work outwards. The fourth section of the first Emulation lecture, speaking of the three so-called Christian virtues of faith, hope and charity, has this to say:

> *'by the doctrines contained in [the VSL] we are taught to believe in the dispensations of divine providence; which belief strengthens our faith, and enables us to ascend the first step [of Jacob's Ladder]. This faith naturally creates in us a hope of becoming partakers of the blessed promises therein recorded; which hope enables us to ascend the second step. But the third and last, being charity, comprehends the whole; and the mason who is possessed of this virtue in its most ample sense may justly be deemed to have attained the summit of his profession; figuratively speaking an ethereal mansion, veiled from mortal eyes by the starry firmament, emblematically depicted in our lodges by seven stars, which have an allusion to as many regularly made masons, without which number no lodge is perfect, neither can any candidate be legally initiated into the Order.*

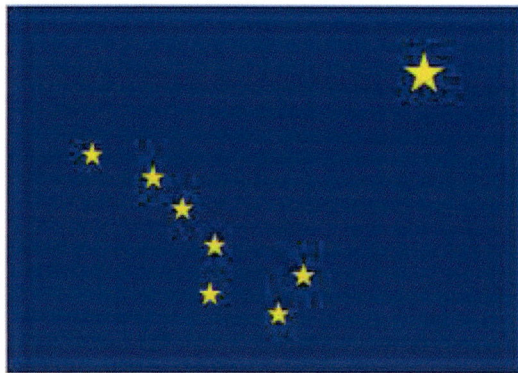

The seven stars in astronomy refer of course to the Great Bear constellation and there is here an interesting connection to French tracing boards of all centuries. Although many French boards will name the cardinal points of the compass, namely north, south, east and west, by their common-usage counterparts of *nord*, *sud*, *est* and *ouest*, it is as common to find the words *septentrion* (north), *midi* (south or midday), *orient* (east) and *occident* (west). The septentrion referred to here is exactly that of the seven-star Great Bear or *Grande Ourse* constellation, which is to be seen in the northern sector of the sky at night, thus bearing a double inference for Freemasons, namely that, apart from denoting the north geographically, it also reminds us of the number seven which has significance in all three degrees.

This constellation is also known by its Latin name, *Ursa Major*, and is visible throughout the year in most of the northern hemisphere. It is dominated by the widely-recognised group of stars known as the Plough, whose last two members point towards the Pole Star in the north and which has mythological significance in numerous cultures. In ancient times the name of the constellation was *Helike*, or 'turning', because it turns around the north pole. In theosophy, it is believed that these seven stars focus the spiritual energy through Sirius, then the sun, then the god of earth and finally through the Masters of the Seven Rays to the human race.

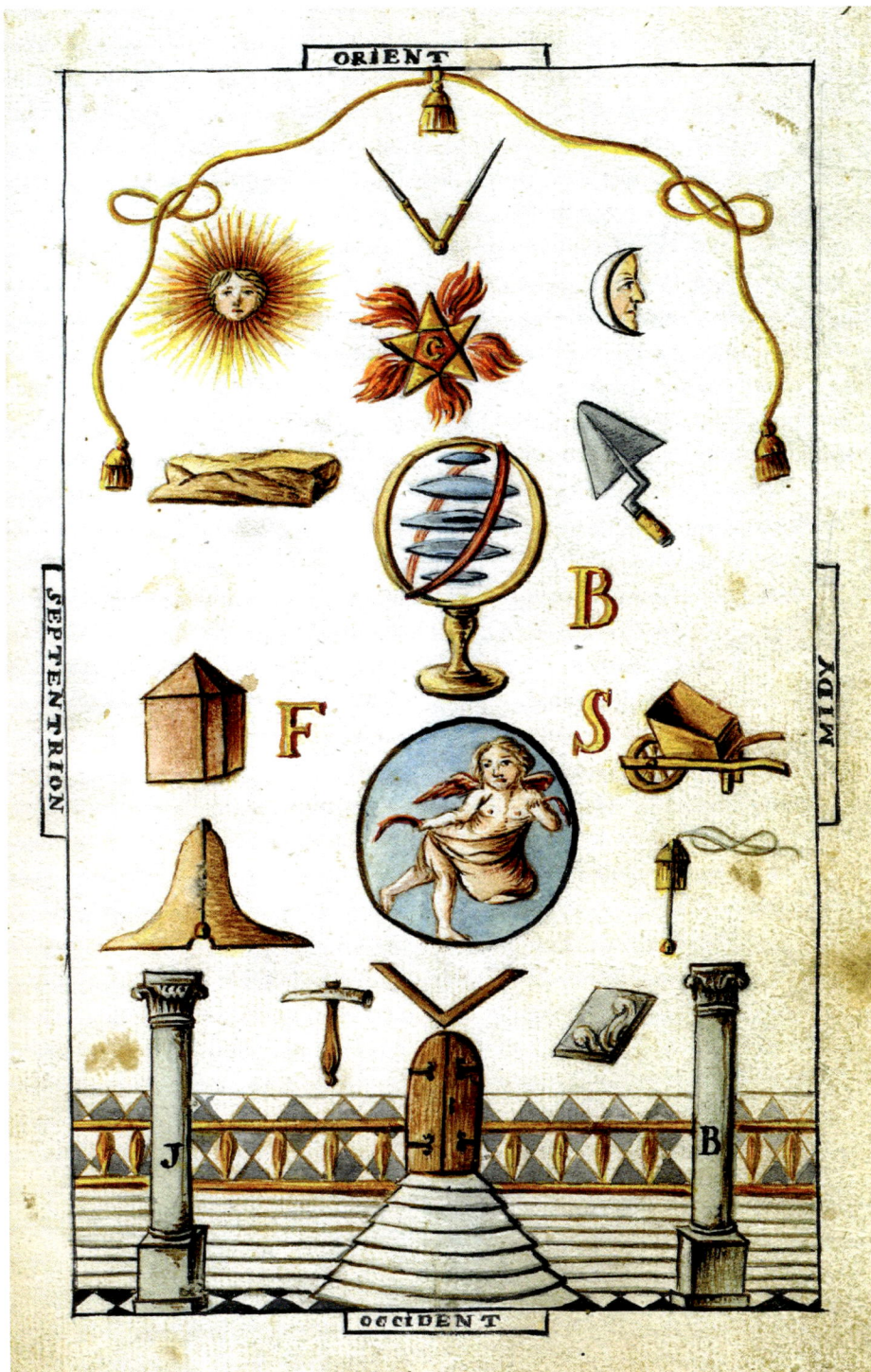

French tracing board of the late 18th/early 19th century. Note the pointed cubic stone, astrolabe, *B[eauté] F[orce]* and *S[agesse]* as beauty, strength and wisdom, and also the use of the word *septentrion* for north.

The reference to the starry firmament in the lecture section quoted above evokes a very interesting resonance with another, more general philosophy of the 18th century. The German philosopher Immanuel Kant said:

Two things fill me with ever increasing wonderment and awe: the starry firmament above me, and the moral law within me.

And at the end of the 19th century, the French astronomer Camille Flammarion wrote:

> *What intelligent being, what being capable of responding to a beautiful sight, can look at the jagged, silvery lunar crescent trembling in the azure sky, even through the weakest of telescopes, and not be struck by it in an intensely pleasurable way, not feel cut off from everyday life here on Earth and transported toward that first stop on celestial journeys? What thoughtful soul could look at brilliant Jupiter with its four attendant satellites, or splendid Saturn encircled by its mysterious ring, or a double star glowing scarlet and sapphire in the infinity of night, and not be filled with a sense of wonder? Yes indeed, if humankind – from humble farmers in the fields and toiling workers in the cities, to teachers, people of independent means, those who have reached the pinnacle of fame or fortune – if they knew what profound inner pleasure awaits those who gaze at the heavens, then France, nay, the whole world, would be covered with telescopes instead of bayonets, thereby promoting universal happiness and peace.*

Think for a moment of our own very humble depiction of seven stars on our tracing boards, and now think of the vastness of the cosmos above and around us. Linking the cosmos and the moral law in the way that Kant did gives us a new perspective: the very nature of our cosmos, vast and almost incomprehensible as it is, reminds us of the greatness of creation, of which our tracing board is but an allegory, and of how boundless ought to be our sense of moral rectitude. But Kant was surely invoking Hermes Trismegistus, mentioned earlier, whose maxim, 'As above, so below,' resonates so clearly with Kant's perception of his relationship to the cosmos.

DIRECTION

And this leads us on to the next almost universal feature of tracing boards: the four cardinal points of the compass. On the face of it, these are mere indications of how to position the board in the Lodge, so that the 'top' of the picture should be oriented towards the Master and the 'bottom' towards the Senior Warden. On these first-degree boards depicting the three lesser lights, the Ionic, Doric and Corinthian pillars, these pillars are roughly oriented towards the positions of the Master and the two Wardens, namely east, west and south, so that, logically, the board would be in the right position when the symbolism of the Lodge was being explained to a candidate.

In fact, the points of the compass have a far-reaching import for Freemasons. As we have seen, the east is the place where the Master is situated, the place of the rising sun, indicative of newness, rebirth and dedication to new tasks. The west is the place where the sun sets, identified by the position of the Senior Warden who is there to close the Lodge and ensure that the brethren, at the end of their day of labour, receive the wages due to them, which are, in Freemasonry, wages of a spiritual worth. Being the position of the setting sun, the west is emblematic also of death, the end of our physical, material journey. For those living in the Northern Hemisphere, the sun will be at its brightest, highest point at midday, therefore due south, and so it is that the Junior Warden is placed in the south. Midday is, of course, the time that workmen pause for refreshment and so it is that the Junior Warden calls the brethren from labour to refreshment, and from refreshment to labour again.

The one point of the compass not often mentioned is the north, and for this too there is a reason. Again for those of us living in the Northern Hemisphere, the sun rises in the east and describes an arc as it rises across the sky to the south at midday, an arc which then descends towards the west so that, figuratively, the north is the least enlightened quadrant. Indeed, in winter, the further north one travels the less light there is. On some old German and Austrian tracing boards, the four points of the compass, north, south, east and west, are shown by the old German words of *Mitnacht* (midnight) in the north, *Mittag* (midday) in the south, *Auffgang* (rising of the sun) in the east and *Nidergang* (setting of the sun) in the west.

WORKING IN STONE

Mural in the Grand Lodge building in New York.

If we go back to the lecture again, regarding the beautiful comparison between the immovable jewels and the furniture of the lodge, we find the following:

The rough ashlar is a stone, rough and unhewn as taken from the quarry, until, by the industry and ingenuity of the workman, it is modelled, wrought into due form, and rendered fit for the intended structure. This represents man in his infant or primitive state, rough and unpolished as that stone, until, by the kind care and attention of his parents or guardians, in giving him a liberal and virtuous education, his mind becomes cultivated, and he is thereby rendered a fit member of civilised society. The perfect ashlar is a stone of a true die or square, fit only to be tried by the square and compasses. This represents man in the decline of years, after a regular, well-spent life in acts of piety and virtue, which can no otherwise be tried and approved than by the square of God's word, and the compass of his own self-convincing conscience.

Mural in the Grand Lodge building in New York.

We are called Freemasons and we are said, if not historically then at least allegorically, to be descended from the operative stonemasons. In consequence, there cannot be many Freemasons who have not grasped the idea that a rough stone is an emblem of a person who has not yet undertaken the task of working at his own nature, his own character, in the spirit of moral and spiritual regeneration, improvement, cultivation. In his book *The Way of the Craftsman*, Kirk MacNulty has the following to say:

> *Although the term is not used during the ceremony, the Entered Apprentice Freemason is represented in the Craft's symbolism as a rough ashlar, or building stone. In the complete symbol, the body of humanity is represented as a quarry from which stone is to be cut to construct a temple to Deity. Ultimately, all of the rock in the quarry is to be incorporated into the building. While the rock remains in the quarry, it is part of the mass, and experiences what the mass experiences. The candidate in the Entered Apprentice degree is about to separate himself out, and to undertake to live his life as an individual, to be a separate stone. It is a step which only he can take; and he can take it only for himself. When he has done it, when he has recognised himself to be an individual, like the rough ashlar cut from the mountain which will never be part of the bedrock again, the Entered Apprentice can never go back. To put it another way, when one has had an insight into his nature, when he has a glimpse of the fact that he really is, inside, at the core of his being the 'Image of God', he can never unknow it. When a person knows what he is, and acknowledges it, he is responsible for himself from that time onward. He will be an individual, with individual responsibility for the rest of his life.*

This then is how we may view the provenance of the rough and unpolished stone, and to understand that by becoming free from the quarry, represented by the act of initiation, we may begin that wonderful work of moulding our moral and spiritual self to make us fit members of society: to enable us to realise our full potential spiritually, morally and indeed physically.

We are to undertake work on that stone, allegorically, in order to smooth it, to level the uneven surface. The first-degree working tools teach us that the second of the working tools, the common gavel

> *represents the force of conscience, which should keep down all vain and unbecoming thoughts …*

and that the third, the chisel

> *points out to us the advantages of education, by which means alone we are rendered fit members of regularly organised society.*

So these working tools are given into our hands to assist in the preparation of the stone, the setting out of the groundwork of our own character, of our own development, morally and spiritually. In the Mystic Charge delivered in the second degree in the Order of Freemasonry Le Droit Humain, the aspirant is exhorted:

> *See to it, as a Fellow Craft, that the world is the better for your smoothing and polishing of the crude stones, and that the Temple we are raising for humanity becomes the fairer for your inclusion among Craftsmen.*

There is, however, an interesting sideline to the smooth or perfect ashlar. In France, the perfect ashlar makes its appearance in the form of a pointed cubic stone.

The French *Pierre Cubique à Pointe* (pointed cubic stone).

A leading French Masonic scholar, Irène Mainguy, has this to say on the subject of this uniquely French Masonic symbol:

> *The four lateral faces of the cube are a reminder of the four cardinal points, while the pyramidion underlines the importance of the zenith … The centre of the square of the base fixes the sacred point … and the vertical axis, rising towards the point of the pyramid, indicates the direction of the ascent to the summit of the mountain, towards which the initiate should strive, and which can be understood as access to pure spirituality.*

The inference here is that the French Freemason has not six faces on which to work but nine, in order to achieve a smooth finish to the whole object. But his finished ashlar points the way more directly to a higher spiritual advancement, a very interesting dimension to consider.

The remaining objects on the tracing board which are more or less common to the four countries mentioned, namely the Square and Compasses, the chequered pavement and the indented or tessellated border, have all been dealt with in the preceding chapters.

What then can we learn from the immovable jewels? The rough and perfect ashlars demonstrate a symbolism which is direct enough and might be said to demonstrate the most basic tenets of Freemasonry. The tracing board, however, displays a much more elaborate and sophisticated symbolism which manifests itself in a pattern of myriad different ways and is open to so much interpretation that it really does repay deeper study. There is plenty of reading to be done on this subject alone and the reading list at the end of this book will give additional guidance to that already given here.

6. ART AND IMAGE

Some objects adorn; others have the appearance of more mundane working tools. We have seen how they may be invested with wide and deep import or allegorical power. If we now move away slightly from the centre and explore the outer circumference of Masonic adornment, we may perhaps trace ways in which the light, the beauty, the artistry, the colour and the exuberance have also become transported to other Masonic objects not quite as central to the Masonic quest as those we have been examining.

Some readers may have purchased this book assuming that it dealt with 'masonic jewels' as most people regard them, namely past paster's jewels, lodge jewels, collar jewels, officers' jewels and so forth. Then there is another way of looking at jewels in a masonic context: jewels of art, sculpture, painting, music, architecture, and we can consider all of these. If we remember that beauty is the third and possibly the most important of the three pillars, namely the Corinthian, then it becomes evident that beauty must predominate in all we do.

And so appealing are the many Masonic ornaments, jewels and artefacts that, in every age, artists have made use of Masonic images to adorn everyday objects. In this way, the humble Square becomes angel's wings and the Square and Compasses motif becomes a fit subject for a chair-back carving.

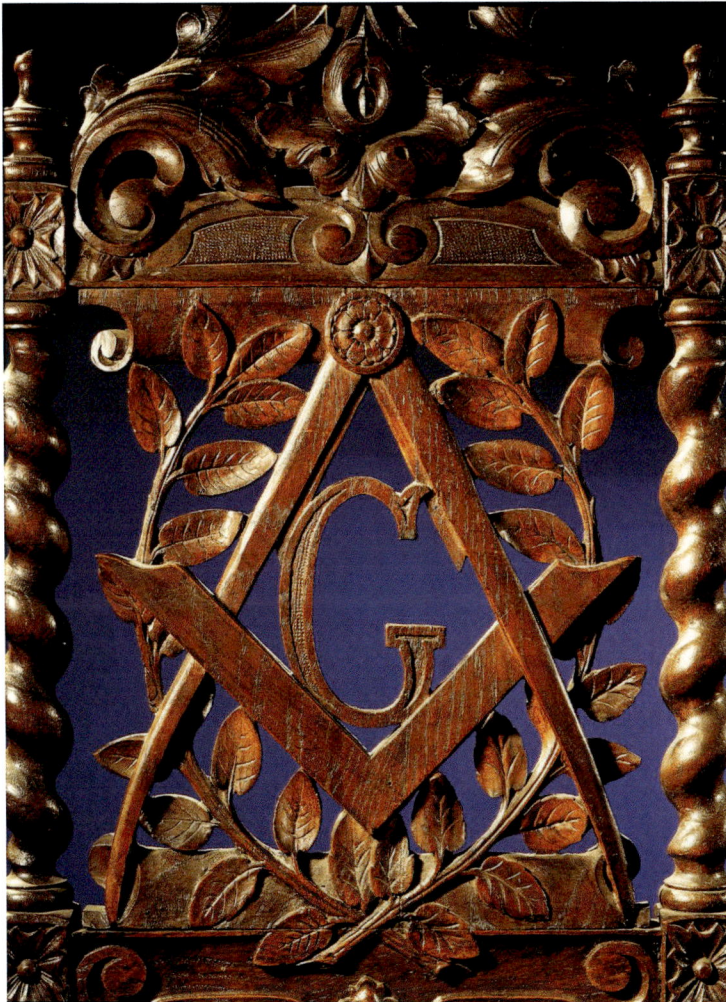

L'AIR.

L'EAV.

LA.TERRE.

LE.FEV.

The four elements – air, water, earth, fire – play an important part in the initiation ceremony in many Masonic rituals worldwide.

The humble Square may take on the form of angels' wings, as on this breast jewel from Le Droit Humain.

We have not had the opportunity to fully explore the many and varied designs of aprons; such a study would merit a book on its own. But in passing we can point out some of the more attractive examples of this genre, some of them sufficiently detailed to act as tracing boards in their own right.

Painted leather apron
of Augustine Harrison.

Old style French
Apron white lambskin,
printed in the early
19th century.

Silk apron, pre-1850.

Leather apron, Howard
Lodge, New York,
dated 1825-1850.

Printed fabric apron,
'Angel and Roses',
pre-1850.

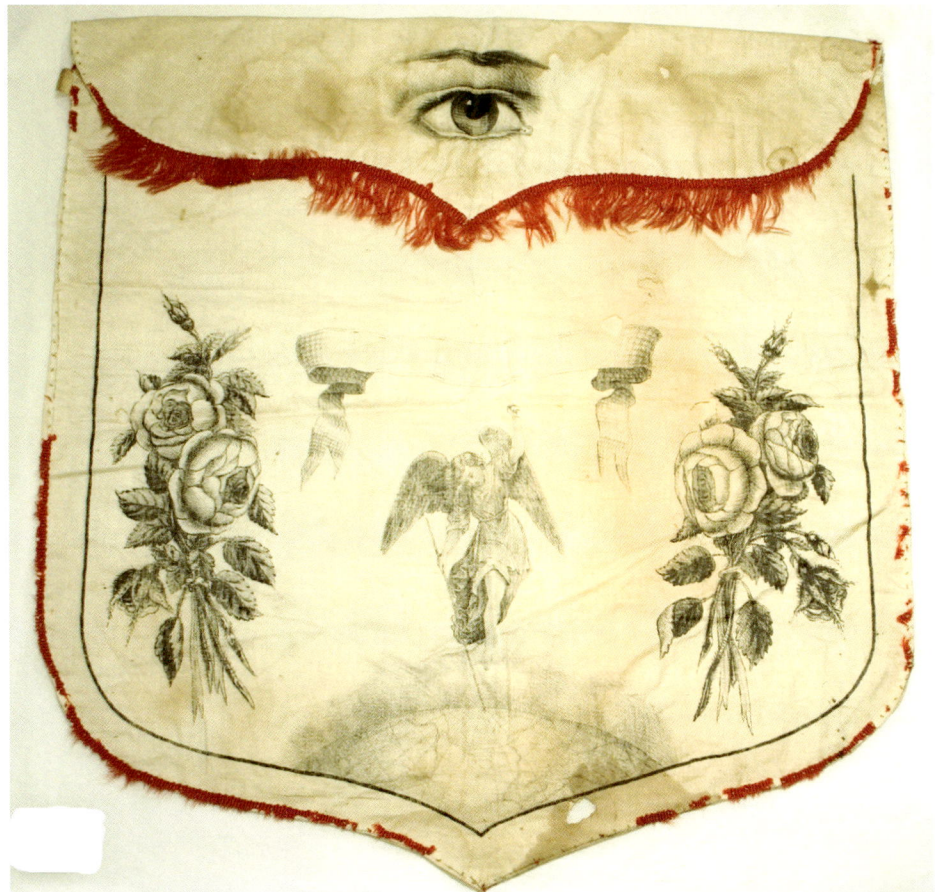

White silk apron with hand-painted symbols, 1860.

Hand-painted silk French Master's apron, dating from the early 19th century.

Compasses, in the guise of collar jewels, or used as ornaments in other ways, evince the most astonishing variety of form and craftsmanship:

Jewel of the first Master of Concord Lodge, New York. 1819.

Compasses from the Kitchener Lodge in England.

Past Master's Jewel of
Benevolent Lodge,
New York, inset with
red and white stones,
1831.

Past Master's Jewel
with double-sided,
three-dimensional sun.
Ocean Lodge,
New York, 1853.

The field of Masonic art is full of various works wrought on porcelain, earthenware or glassware:

Earthenware dish belonging to the lodge Libération, Nevers, France, 2000.

Earthenware plate belonging to the lodge Libération, Nevers, France, 2000.

Plate made by François Devillaire of Liré, France,
1831.

Rectangular ceramic plaque depicting the tracing
board, dating from the mid-18th century,
Moustiers, France.

Cup in painted and gilded
porcelain, 1858.

Gilded Bohemian glass goblet.

And one particularly fine example of an openwork bronze Grand Orient de France jewel, showing Square, Compasses and Blazing Star in a compact design.

It would be a mistake to suppose that Masonic symbolism has grown up alongside other systems and organisations without influencing them, or those systems in turn influencing Freemasonry. There are ample indications that Masonic ritual and symbolism and the world's great religions have influenced each other over the centuries. To take one of the central Masonic symbols, the Blazing Star, we find many references to this in Christian symbolism and practice. A number of stained glass windows in Christian churches exhibit traces of five-pointed and six-pointed stars similar to those used as Blazing Stars in Masonic symbolism.

French Master's jewel from the 19th century onwards.

Two Rose Windows in the Cathedral of Amiens, France, both showing the five-pointed star.

Detail from a window
in Notre Dame, Paris.

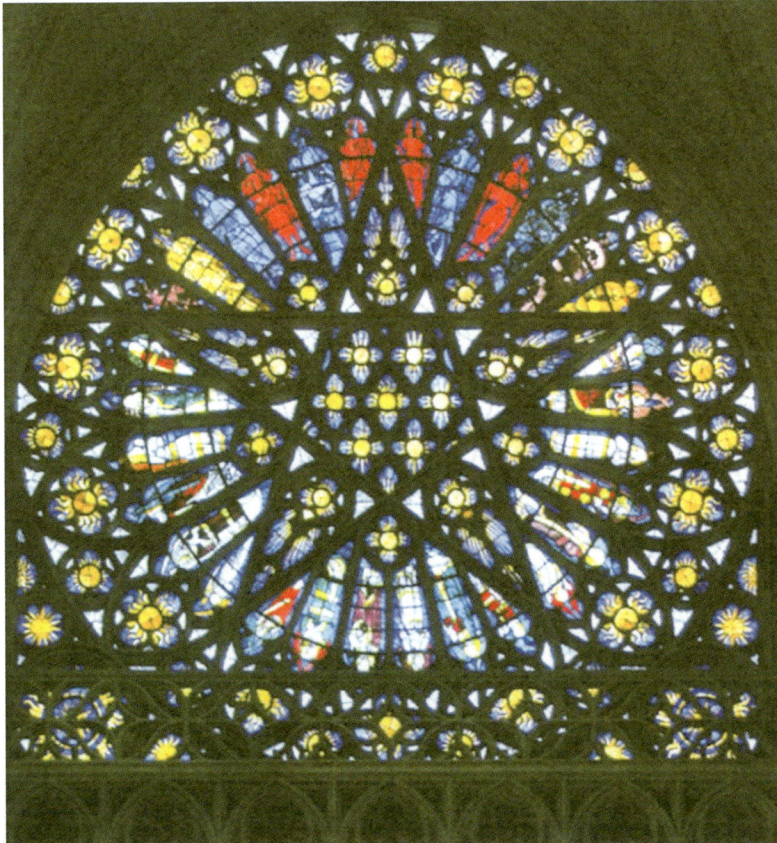

A Rose Window in the Abbey of St Ouen in
Rouen, showing the five-pointed star.

And, if further proof were needed of the connections between church architecture and Masonic symbolism, one would look no further than the two splendid pillars flanking the west entrance to the Karlskirche in Vienna.

From such grandiose ornaments to this intricate and charming mother-of-pearl inlay box, the influence of Masonic symbolism surrounds our world and is an integral part of it, whether as active symbols, as described in the foregoing chapters, or simply as adornment to bring light and beauty into our lives. To quote Masonic ritual once more:

May His beauty dwell in our hearts.

FURTHER READING

The English-speaking reader should not be put off by the non-English language titles referenced here, which are all richly illustrated.

Curl, James Stevens, *The Art and Architecture of Freemasonry*, Batsford, 1991. ISBN 0 7134 5827 5

Dyer, Colin F.W., *Symbolism in Craft Freemasonry*, Lewis Masonic, 1976. ISBN 0 85318 233 7

Cross, Jeremy, *The True Masonic Chart, or Hieroglyphic Monitor*, first published in New Haven, Connecticut, 1819.

Feddersen, Klaus C.F., *Arbeitstafel in der Freimaurerei*, Quatuor Coronati Lodge, Bayreuth, Germany.

Graves, Alun, *Tiles and Tilework*, V&A Publications, 2002. ISBN 1 85177 345 2

Jardin, Dominique, *Voyages dans les Tableaux de Loge*, Jean-Cyrille Godefroy, 2011. ISBN 978 2 86553 230 8

The Lectures in the Three Degrees in Craft Masonry, Lewis Masonic. ISBN 978 0 85318 328 0

MacNulty, W. Kirk, *Freemasonry – A Journey through Ritual and Symbol*, Thames and Hudson, 1991. ISBN 0 500 81037 0

MacNulty, W. Kirk, *The Way of the Craftsman*, Central Regalia, 2002. ISBN 0 954 2516 0 1

MacNulty, W. Kirk, *Freemasonry – Symbols, Secrets, Significance*, Thames and Hudson, 2006. ISBN 978 0 500 51302 6

Marcos, Mollier, Morillon and Robillot, *Le Grand Livre Illustré du Patrimoine Maçonnique*, Le Cherche Midi, 2011. ISBN 978 2 7491 1782 9

Mainguy, Irène, *La Symbolique Maçonnique du Troisième Millénaire*, Editions Dervy, 2006. ISBN 978 2 84454 116 1

Rees, Julian, *Making Light – a Handbook for Freemasons*, Lewis Masonic, 2006. ISBN 0 85318 253 1

Rees, Julian, *Tracing Boards of the Three Degrees in Craft Freemasonry Explained*, Lewis Masonic, 2009. ISBN 978 0 853183 34 1

Trescass, Jacques, *L'Étoile Flamboyante*, Éditions Véga, 2011. ISBN 978 2 85829 686 6

Webb, Thomas Smith, *Freemason's Monitor or Illustrations of Masonry*, first published in Cincinnati, Ohio, 1859.

INDEX

WS - #0109 - 270923 - C66 - 280/215/6 - PB - 9780853184126 - Gloss Lamination